AME

ENSLAVED & DEPENDENT

How to reclaim your personal financial freedom

Joseph M. Murtagh

Royal Fireworks Press
Unionville, New York

Printed by Royal Fireworks

Cover design by A&E Advertising

First Edition, 2000

ISBN: 0-89824-973-2

Table of Contents

Acknowledgments

Introduction — 1

Chapter I — 6
Back To The Future

Chapter II — 12
Independence

Chapter III — 18
Overspending

Chapter IV — 23
Spending It All

Chapter V — 28
Spending It After You Pay Yourself First

Chapter VI — 35
The Great Crossover

Chapter VII — 41
What Do I Do With The Money?

Chapter VIII — 46
Earn The Right To Be An Investor

Chapter IX — 51
So Now You're An Investor

Chapter X — 57
What About Investment Taxes And Inflation?

Chapter XI   67

    I'm Too Poor To Become Financially Independent

Chapter XII   75

    Solid Middle Class

Chapter XIII   81

    Affluence Or Looking Good On The Outside

Chapter XIV   87

    For The Top 2%. . . The Wealthy

Epilogue   95

About the Author   100

How to Contact Us   101

Appendix A   102

Appendix B   103

Footnotes   104

Acknowledgments

Without the help of a great team of people this book would not be possible. The encouragement and support of my family, especially my wife Maryanna with her many suggestions and assistance in formatting, has been wonderful.

The cover ideas and suggestions by my great friend and mentor, Harold Card, coupled with the cover design by Edison and Ada Guzman make this a high impact product.

The editing of the manuscript by my friends Bob Riemann and Marcy Berchtold, along with suggestions from Frank Fevoli and support from Jack Paluszek, Mike Smith, and other members of "the Consultants Committee" too numerous to mention, is very appreciated.

Special thanks to the Boy Scouts of America, my first scout master Bob Mitchell and the United States Jaycees for such positive influence in shaping my life as a volunteer and citizen of this great country.

Finally, thank you, America, for providing me, my family and friends, all of us... with the opportunity to be free and do with our lives whatever we choose. May we all exercise this "power of choice"... with the greatest of care.

America 2000
Enslaved & Dependent

We live in the world's greatest country. We have freedoms that are enjoyed by no other people on earth. Nevertheless, many of us are still in bondage. How can this be?

Americans of earlier generations were truly independent. They provided for themselves by putting money away for a rainy day and also cared for the less fortunate. Instead of government helping people, people helped people.

This sense of responsibility was possible because Americans of yesterday knew the art of saving. Many of us don't. We need to rethink our spending habits, to establish our own Financial Independence and to free ourselves from the need for government programs, such as Medicare and Social Security.

In this book you will find step by step procedures to free you from the bondage of dependence on unreliable government programs. Not far from you are housing projects, slum neighborhoods, and failed public schools.

You will learn how to maintain your lifestyle during your retirement years, provide for children's education and aid your parents in their golden years.

Learn to feel better about yourself and recapture the destiny of your community. Learn how to become confident and self-assured about your financial future.

What better gift could you give to your children than the living example of how to achieve financial independence? It is a lesson they will never forget.

See how you can achieve your financial goals, beginning where you are today. This book is not full of theories. It is filled with practical advice, spelled out in easy steps. It's your future, make it the best one possible!

Introduction

We live in the world's greatest country. We have freedoms that are enjoyed by no other people on earth. Nevertheless, many of us are still in bondage. How can this be?

During the Great Depression, the federal government set up temporary social programs designed to help U.S. citizens hit hard by economic disaster that left many families without money to buy food.

Since then, these special programs, designed for a specific economic problem, have grown into "entitlements," and many citizens have become dependent on big government support. They have forgotten the independent ways of their ancestors.

No one believed Joseph Schumpiter, economist and author of *Capitalism, Socialism and Democracy,* who in the 1940's predicted the fall of Communism in Eastern Europe by 1980, yet he was only off by 10 years. He also predicted that workers in the capitalist society would vote in Communism.

Americans of earlier generations were truly independent because they provided for themselves by putting money away for a rainy day. They enjoyed a level of independence that few have today, because they were not only able to care for themselves but were able to help those who were less fortunate.

Instead of government helping people, people helped people. Those who did well financially, instead of being highly taxed (no income tax existed until 1913), assisted in providing for their own communities needs, building schools, orphanages and hospitals.

This native sense of responsibility, not only for one-self but also for others, was possible because those Americans of yesterday knew the art of saving. It was something they absorbed from the example of their parents.

For many of us living today, those lessons were not taught to us as children. Now, as an adult, you have to rethink your spending habits to establish your own "financial independence" and to free yourself from bondage to government programs such as Medicare and Social Security. A look around shows you the failure of many previous, well-intended government programs and their devastating results.

Not far from you there are housing projects, slum neighborhoods, and failed public schools. It's not too late to assume personal responsibility for your financial freedom. Remember, history shows that relying on government often leads to disaster. This book will show you the way out of this unreliable governmental dependency regardless of your current circumstances.

Is such a change possible? Yes, it is. In this book, you will find step-by-step procedures that will free you from the bondage of dependence on government programs. You will be able to maintain your lifestyle during your retirement years. You will be able to finance the education of your children and aid your parents in their golden years.

"But I have only enough money to just meet my monthly bills." Join the club. In today's America, it is popular to "spend all you earn." Few have money to set aside. Or so we believe.

However, there is an answer to this perplexing dilemma. It is the secret that made America great. It is not an easy answer, but it is an answer. Here is the difficult part. You have to learn how to change your spending habits. This book will help.

To do this, you must first thoroughly understand why you handle your finances the way you do. Be non-judgmental. Look at your family budget honestly (Appendix A). This is the only way you can comprehend how the bad habits you have acquired keep you in bondage.

Many Americans today are much like the coal miners of old who were tied to the company store. The mine owners knew that if they kept most of their workers constantly in debt and everyone relying on the company store for their needs, they would never be able to leave the mines.

Today, many of us are tied, not to mines but to habits...bad habits...that keep us from ever reaching our financial goals. We are enslaved and rely on "the government store" to provide for our individual, family, and community needs. We feel helpless and dependent.

Learn how to break those bonds. Learn how to feel better about yourself and recapture the destiny of your community. Learn how to become confident and self-assured about your financial future. What better gift could you give to your children than being a living example of how to achieve financial independence? It is a lesson they will never forget.

But don't take my word for it. Read on and see how you can achieve your financial goals step-by-step, beginning where you are today. This book is not full of theories. It is filled with practical advice, spelled out in easy steps.

The book details:

1.   How your present habits are hurting you.

2.   Why you should change.

3.   How you can change.

4.   The lasting benefits of financial freedom for yourself, your family, and community...for generations to come.

The first step is to become convinced that financial independence and freedom from reliance on government is possible for you, your family, and your community. Next, start following the simple steps, one at a time, as outlined in this book.

There is even more. Many of the ills of today are caused by big government bureaucrats meddling in our lives. From the local schools to taking care of the poor and elderly, government is pulling the strings...because it controls the money.

But wait. That's our money. We should be the ones calling the shots in our communities, and we can! But not if we as individuals have no financial resources.

In the final chapters, this book presents a vision of how "financially independent" citizens can make a difference in the way we live. You as an individual can take back the control of your neighborhood, a responsibility that has been usurped by big government.

It is a grand vision, and America, starting with the Declaration of Independence, is the product of many past grand visions. Remember that the longest journey begins with a single step. Read on, and rediscover the **secret of financial independence.** "We have been there before."

Chapter I

Back to the Future

STEVEN FORBES
"Rights carry with them duties and responsibilities."

Let's look at America's most recent report card and start with the average grade F. "How so?" you ask. According to AARP recent statistics[1], out of every 100 people who retire in this country today, only two are wealthy and another five could live without any government assistance. Fifteen more have achieved "subsidized independence" (could not maintain lifestyle if government assistance vanished), and the remaining 78 are totally dependent on government programs and charity for their very existence.

If ever we needed a plan for free individuals living in strong and vital communities, self-governing and self-supporting, it is now. Fortunately, we still have a choice. We can use our freedom and ingenuity, coupled with some careful personal planning, to build the kind of communities we want while enjoying more income for ourselves and leaving more for our heirs. Only by becoming personally financially free, can we as a society shed the chains of government bondage, reclaim our personal financial freedom, and then our community independence.

A look back at our own national past exemplifies individuals and local communities taking care of themselves. It happened through the efforts of interdependent and free citizens working together through leagues, associations, boards, councils, churches, schools, social clubs, hospitals, children's groups, colleges, foundations and dozens of other organizations that we call charities. These organizations made the communities of yesterday…our parents' and grandparents' neighborhoods, towns and villages…strong and vital. During this same period, there were only minimal taxes.

Looking back at those communities of the past, we can see just why they worked and how we can make them work again. As recently as 40 years ago, farmers who had lost their barns to fire or a storm were joined by neighbors who came to help with a barn raising. Throughout the day, the whole community pitched in, some providing lumber, some tools, still others skills…carpentry, cooking, baby-sitting. By day's end, the new barn stood, and the neighbors returned to their homes.

Although urban needs were different, it was much the same in the cities. The answer was the same: neighbors giving, volunteering, and sharing. As time went on, leagues, associations, societies, foundations, and all kinds of groups were formed to provide clothing, food, shelter, education, medical care, and a host of other needs. The focus was never on a "hand out," but rather, a "hand up," neighbors helping neighbors to become independent citizens.

This was a way of life everywhere in our nation, a way of life that struck foreigners as extraordinary. Visitors from Europe had never seen anything quite like our unique mixture of charity, personal civic responsibility, and a healthy skepticism of any government larger than the local town council.

That tradition of meeting our own needs as individuals, communities, and sovereign states held fast in America and survived every kind of social and natural challenge:

wars (including our Civil War), epidemics, and natural disasters. Through all these disasters, families and neighbors, working individually and collectively, continued to help each other.

Because individuals, families, and local communities were meeting their own needs all this time, the government remained small. There was no income tax until 1913.

Then the Depression struck, bringing poverty to Americans everywhere. To restore prosperity, government created the New Deal. With this new program, government now played the role of problem-solver on a national scale. Its philosophy was: "If people and local communities cannot handle their own problems, we will." It is a role that has continued to this day and has changed the way we think about government and the very way we live.

The Great Depression of 1929 not only caused food lines, massive unemployment, and excruciatingly painful financial hardship for the nation, **it broke the independent spirit and self-confidence of the American people. We have never recovered.**

Government launched the "New Deal" and, coupled with many other factors, individuals and families began to recover, and local economies began to grow. Americans were ready to return to their traditional community-centered way of life. The federal government, people said, had saved the nation, and could now dismantle itself. The top income tax rate rose from 7% in 1913 to 78% in 1938.

Instead, the federal government began to grow and, as it grew, we became more dependent on it instead of relying on ourselves and our neighbors as we had in the past.

For a long time, however, no one seemed to notice. The top tax rate reached 90% in 1960.

Then, in the '70's, people began to notice that even though the federal government was getting bigger, local communities were not prospering. We began to wonder if the federal government was really the answer to all our problems…they responded with "tax cuts."

Our government is notorious for "smoke and mirror games." The Tax Foundation has been reporting on "Tax Freedom Day"(Appendix B)$_2$ for generations, and reports about the day that the average American is done paying all taxes and begins to work for himself or herself. In 1960, the maximum federal tax rate was 90% and "Tax Freedom Day" was April 11th. This year, the maximum federal rate is 39.6%, and "Tax Freedom Day" was postponed until the 3rd of May.

There is a better answer from our forefathers. They proved that individual citizens and their communities, re-lying on their own resources, including the will, money, and energy of their people, along with the good work of their charitable organizations, could meet their own needs and do a better job than government.

We are beginning to see citizens return to their local charities and renew their commitment of support throughout the nation's communities, and government is now contract-ing with charitable organizations to provide some human services.

We have seen a new attitude in the federal govern-ment as well, with Congress slashing the deficit, promising to close down whole departments, and balance the budget.

Clearly, something has changed and now, with a record surplus, huge new spending plans are proposed.

We live in the only country in the world where the average citizen drives a bank-financed car on a bond-financed highway on credit card gasoline on his way to a furniture store to make an installment purchase to fill his S&L-mortgaged home. Average families in America today can't have fun on vacation unless they're doing something that they can't afford.

At its zenith, every great civilization in history, every "golden age," has experienced the same core symptoms that we face in America today...loss of moral values, government out of control, and a population looking to others to solve its problems.

National commentator Paul Harvey said[3], "How would you like to work for a company which has fewer than 600 employees. Of those 600 employees...29 have been accused of spousal abuse...7 have been arrested for fraud...19 have been accused of writing bad checks...117 have bankrupted at least two businesses...3 have been arrested for assault...71 can't get a credit card because of bad credit...14 have been arrested on drug related charges... 8 have been arrested for shoplifting...21 are current defendants in lawsuits. And in 1998 alone, 84 were stopped for drunk driving. That company is the United States Congress."

The histories of all great civilizations indicate that they have come and gone because of internal corruption (campaign finance reform) coupled with citizens apathy, low achievement drive, complacency, and lack of accountability. A government that robs Peter to pay Paul can always depend on the support of Paul.

In order to restore our freedom and control our personal, family and community lives, we must first free ourselves from the dependence we now have on government programs. To do this, each of us must become personally financially independent. As Leo Tolstoy once said, *"Many are willing to change the world...few to change themselves."*

Chapter II

Independence

GEORGE BERNARD SHAW
"Success comes from taking the path of maximum advantage, not least resistance."

What is personal financial independence, financial freedom? It's something that is both different for everyone...yet the same for us all.

It's different for everyone because it's a function directly related to lifestyle. Someone may be financially independent with an income of $25,000 per year while another may not be with an income of $25,000 per month.

Independence is the same for everyone. When you accumulate assets that, without Social Security and government benefits, generate enough income to fund your lifestyle, adjusting for both inflation and taxes, you're financially independent.

There are many reading this book who could be financially independent with $25,000 or $50,000 per year and just as many who need $100,000 to do the trick. Some of you need $250,000 and a few need more...much more. Why?

Lifestyle is the answer and, once you're used to one lifestyle, it's very, very difficult to go back to something less. The paradox is that it's lifestyle that keeps virtually everyone from ever becoming financially independent. Remember, only 7 out of every 100 persons in America today are free of financial worry…truly independent.

You see, there are only **three** types of **financial personalities** in this world: **"overspenders," "spend it all,"** and **"spend it after I paid myself first."** If you're the third type, move on to Chapters XII and beyond as you're either already financially independent or well on your way.

An "overspender personality" spends more than he makes. A "spend it all person" spends every last penny he makes. Only the "spend it after I pay myself first personality" spends less than he makes and, as a result, is paying himself first all the time.

When you got out of bed today, you didn't consciously think about getting dressed. You just got dressed. You may have consciously thought about what to wear but you got dressed out of habit. You didn't try to put your pants on over your head or put your shoes on the wrong feet, but you have seen little children do that because they haven't yet formed the habit of dressing. You have already formed **financial habits,** and two of the three habit choices lead to disaster.

The vast majority $(93\%)_1$ of retired Americans today are not financially independent, yet never had a problem going on vacation or buying a new car. The student, who graduates from high school today and does not continue education, will have over \$1,000,000 earned and spent during his working lifetime.

A great-grandfather who came to America from Europe tells this high school student his story. "After being processed at Ellis Island$_2$, I went into a cafeteria in New

York City to get something to eat. I sat down at an empty table and waited for someone to take my order.

Of course, nobody did. Finally, a man with a tray full of food sat down opposite me and told me how things worked."

"Start at the end," he said, "and just go along and pick out what you want. At the other end, they'll tell you how much to pay for it." " I soon learned that's how everything works in America," Great-grandpa told the new graduate.

"Life is a cafeteria here," Great-grandpa continued. "You can get anything you want as long as you're willing to pay the price. You even can get success. But you'll never get it if you wait for someone to bring it to you. You have to get up and get it yourself."

If that same student would start at age 18 to save and then begin to invest as little as $20 per week, do you have any idea what he would be worth at age 65? Take a guess. One "Andrew Jackson"($20) a week over 50 weeks is $1,000 each year, so over the 47 working years if the money were put under the mattress you would have $47,000.

As you'll see later, by properly saving and then investing, the money will compound and grow, earning you more money over time. You see, there are only two ways of earning money: you at work, and your money at work. Financially free people have always used both methods.

Albert Einstein said, "Of all the laws I discovered during my life, the law of compounding interest was the most amazing." Now, you take a guess as to how much this 18-year-old will have at age 65. You're right, before you can get the answer, you must know what rate the money will earn when invested. Over the long-term (since 1929), conservative U.S. stock investments have averaged 10 to 12 percent. That doesn't guarantee that's what you'll average, but let's use it as a guide.

Our recent graduate certainly has a long term to invest, so let's start off with 10 and then take a look at what happens when going to 12 percent. If the investment is made at the end of each year, and our student earns an average of 10 percent, it will grow to $871,975. That's a total of $47,000 paid in at a rate of $1,000 per year, compounding at 10% per year for 47 years. Amazing, isn't it?

Now, if our student waits 2 years to get started and saves $1,000 for 45 years and earns the same 10 percent each year...guess what the wait will cost? "Well, $2,000 of course," you say. Would you believe $153,070!

That brings us to the second most important point about financial success....*time.* By waiting just two years we had less time for the money to compound, and at age 65 saving the same $1,000 per year, but now for two fewer years, our student has $718,905, not $871,975. Get started now, and put what Einstein called the "most amazing discovery of the twentieth century" to work for you. Even if you're 65, you have a life expectancy of probably 20 years or perhaps even more.

Before we leave this section, if our student got 12 instead of 10 percent for 47 years, the $1,000 per year would grow to $1,705,884 and, if this investment were delayed two years, it would be $1,358,230. The cost of waiting would be not $2,000, but all the earnings that could have accrued, or in this case, $347,654…so get started today!

Basic financial planning and business education are important because the lack of them has brought about these startling results today: **According to AARP in its 1999 report**[3]: *A Profile Of Older Americans* based on those 65 and older…"36% reported income of less than $10,000 and only 22% earned $25,000 or more. The **median income was $13,768** and the national poverty level for a family of four is $16,000. The median net worth was $86,300 with the majority of that attributable to home ownership. 79% of those surveyed owned their home free and clear."

Home ownership represents the vast majority of the net worth of those over 65 today, and there is a lesson for us here. Buying a home requires the discipline of making a payment every month and not taking the money back out. 80% of today's retirees have less than $600 in cash assets. Only seven percent of the U.S. population who retire today are financially independent. The rest rely on government benefits or charity.

We live in a free country where we are all allowed to become anything we want and earn and save as much as we would like, yet only seven percent of our population leave bondage and the rest of us are dependent on government or charity. Why? Bad habits…and little or no financial education.

What benefit is it to live in a free country if we never enjoy the financial freedom because of not achieving independence from government and charity? To be free, truly free, we must be financially independent…and every reader can.

Remember, statistics show that out of every 100 Americans retired today, only 2 are wealthy, another 5 are financially independent and 15 are subsidized independents (if Social Security were cut off they would be destitute). The remaining 78 are totally dependent on charity or government programs. Conclusion…**most people have very bad financial habits!**

Now that you have recognized the "financial habit" that you currently are in, let's begin to study it further and either change to a "spend it after I pay myself first" or, if you're already personally financially independent, move forward to chapter XII and consider taking more responsibility for the wealth that you already have. Remember Great-grandpa's story. "Nobody is going to bring it to you, you have to get up and get it yourself."

Chapter III

Overspending

JAMES JOYCE
"Mistakes are the portals of discovery."

You see, if you're "overspending," you're in the habit of spending more than you make. Remember back 10 years ago. Where did you live? What kind of car did you drive? How often did you eat out? What type of restaurants did you go to? How much were you making ten years ago?

It doesn't matter what social class you're part of, poor, middle class, or affluent. If you're in the **overspending habit,** you'll never achieve financial freedom and independence. Most of you live under the illusion that making more money will solve your problem. Wrong! As you make more you are in the habit of continuing to spend more than you make.

Most of you are making more than you did 10 years ago, probably a lot more, but it is still not enough because you're spending more. You're not alone. Every day the news is filled with very successful entertainers and sports figures who are filing for bankruptcy because they, like you, spend more than they make. Bad habits are difficult to change...but the results are worth the effort.

Ben Franklin[1] was not always the wise and restrained man we now picture him as being. When he was young, he was often brash, rude, and intolerant of the weakness of others. He was often critical and would tell people to their faces what was wrong with them.

In his youth, he created many enemies, but later in life Franklin became so good at handling people that he was made Ambassador to France. When asked the secret of his success in getting along with others, "I will speak ill of no man," he answered, "and speak all the good I know of everybody." He changed a destructive habit, and you can too.

We laugh and say only the U.S. Government can spend more than it makes. That is wrong too. No government, business or person can survive over the long term when they spend more than they make. The Soviet Union is a recent example, and history shows that all the great civilizations of the past and "Ancient Golden Ages" ended due, in great part, to this same problem.

As an overspender you are carrying debt and this creates a dual challenge because not only must you start to pay yourself first, but you must address and eliminate all debt except your home mortgage if you have one. To do this successfully, you need a plan and the discipline to stick with it.

First you must stop accumulating more debt and begin to pay off all that you have. Do not ignore any creditor, but rather send each a letter explaining your situation and the plan that you have to pay everyone off. Then tell them you will send them a check for a specific amount every month and that your first payment is enclosed.

While your creditors may not like this they will, for the most part, accept your proposal, as they don't want to incur time and expense for other collection proceedings. Most collection agencies get one-third of what they collect and your creditor will be happier with the full amount from you even though it may take a long time. You *must* send your check on time every month.

As a next step you must do a detailed budget (Appendix A) that includes provisions for adequate life, disability, and health care insurance. Having done that you must simply make a commitment to:

A. Save 10% of all that's made.

B. Use 20% for debt payment.

Our 40th President, Ronald Reagan[2], once said: " The character that takes command in moments of crucial choices has already been determined. It has been determined by a thousand other choices made earlier in seemingly unimportant moments. It has been determined by all the "little" choices of years past...by all those times when the voice of conscience was at war with the voice of temptation...whispering the lie that "it really doesn't matter." It has been determined by all the day-to-day decisions made when life seemed easy and crisis seemed far away...the decision that, piece by piece, bit by bit, developed habits of discipline or of laziness; habits of self-sacrifice or of self-indulgence; habits of duty and honor and integrity...or dishonor and shame." Begin now to change the old habit.

Out of the 10% that is saved, first accumulate enough to cover 6 months of living expenses; the rest must be invested for your long-term financial freedom. Always keep 6 months of expenses in a savings or money market account for emergencies or opportunities. If any of it is spent, it must be replaced immediately. The 10% that is invested must never be spent and is earmarked for retirement.

The 20% is to pay debt, and each creditor is to receive a note with a check as described above. If you will tenaciously follow this simple plan, you will have:

1.   An instant estate, if you die before creating adequate family security.

2.   Adequate income to cover living expenses in the event of disability.

3.   A savings account and health insurance benefits.

4.   Paid yourself first.

5.   An orderly debt repayment program.

6.   70% of your income to live on; to pay your taxes, to run the house and for entertainment.

7.   Laid the foundation for long-term financial success and be well on your way to achieving personal financial independence.

So why not set the goal to change a habit that is fast leading you to dependence and a lifelong fear that the government programs you rely upon may go away. By adopting and sticking to this simple plan, you will do six very important things for yourself and family because...

1.   Change will occur anyway...for better or worse.

2.   You will create a future where opportunities become achievements.

3.   Your direction will be established and fears overpowered.

4.   Your focus will be fixed and wasteholes of negative energy drains will be plugged.

5.   Your aim will be excellence and mediocrity will be rejected.

6.   Your hope will be renewed and optimism will blossom.

The great American writer, Mark Twain, said, *"Make it a point to do something every day that you don't want to do. This is the golden rule for acquiring the habit of doing your duty without pain."*

Chapter IV

Spending It All

THOMAS CARLYLE

"The greatest of faults is to be conscious of none."

If you're "spending it all," you'll never achieve financial independence either...you just won't go bankrupt as fast. Going back ten years, what kind of vacations did you take? How many suits did you own and how much did you pay for each? How much were you making and spending ten years ago?

For those in the habit of "spending everything" they make, making more money doesn't help because the habit demands that you **spend it all**. Your advantage is you won't go broke until later, sometime after you retire. Why?

Your habit won't allow you to put something away for later. Look back at your life and check it out. If you have ever put some away for later...the later came sooner than expected. For some of you, it was a special treat you deserved for working so hard, a vacation, a new car, or upgrading your wardrobe.

Others have "higher reasons"...your daughter only gets married once, your son shouldn't come out of college with debt, or the kids need help getting started in life. Maybe Mom and Dad need help, or Uncle Harry is ill.

It doesn't matter why you continue the habit of "break-even spending" because the long-term result is always the same. You will be dependent on Social Security and Medicare at best and, at worst, go completely broke during retirement after selling much of what you accumulated during life (like your home & second home) and moving to a different neighborhood. It is not a matter of if… but simply of when.

In the old days of the West[1], ranchers would sometimes take a wild horse that they could not break, tie it to a little burro, and turn them loose. Before long, the bucking horse would disappear over the desert horizon, dragging the helpless burro behind.

Days would pass, but eventually the odd couple would reappear. The little burro would come first, with the submissive steed in tow.

What went on out on the range always brought the same result. The horse would buck and kick and pitch and pull, but the burro, willing or not, would hang on. Finally the steed would become exhausted, and at some point the burro would take control.

When you spend all you make, you're acting like the unbroken horse and you are temporarily in charge of what is going on. The burro is like the government who knows that it will eventually be in charge, willing or not, and taxes those working to support the out-of-control behaviors of the soon-to-be broke and dependent horses of our country.

What's wrong with dependence on Social Security and Medicare, you ask? If you're not independent and free, does it matter whether you're a slave to a southern plantation owner, indentured to the Generals…Electric, Dynamics, Motors…, a servant in the palace of the king, or hoping that the U.S. government will continue Social Security and

Medicare benefits while watching how difficult it is for your children who must, through their ever increasing taxes, support these "social programs"?

Will Social Security and Medicare be there when you need them and even if they are, do you want your children paying 30 or even 40 percent of their earnings to support you? In 1950, there were 16.5 workers for each one drawing benefits; today there are four workers for each one drawing benefits and, between 2010 and 2030, there will be only two workers for each one drawing benefits.

The tab for each one working today is 15.3% of pay between employee and employer, and just to stay even when there are only two workers for each retiree, that rate would have to double to 30.6%. The average life expectancy of a person retiring today at 65 is 20 years, and we haven't begun to see the life expectancy increases that will come from biotechnology.

All social programs, by the way, exist because of the bad habits we have formed in this great and free country. The subsidy du jour, be it Social Security, Food Stamps, Low Income Housing, Medicaid, Government Grants, Business and Agricultural Subsidies, University Research Grants, and assistance of all types, exists because we have formed the habit of abdicating our personal responsibility and delegating it to Government.

We must embrace our personal responsibility to be financially independent and live within our means. For those providing employment, you must be building businesses successful enough to provide a living, not a minimum wage. Failure to assume this responsibility has caused government intervention, which has enslaved 93 out of every 100 retired Americans today.

If you can't break these old habits and **pay yourself first**, the game is over...you can't win. You will always be concerned that this government program or that one will be eliminated and never live a day where, in the back of your mind, there isn't financial concern about something. The only way to financial independence is to break the old habit of spending it all, and pay yourself first.

In ancient times$_2$, a king had a boulder placed on a roadway. Then he hid himself and watched to see if anyone would remove the huge rock. Some of the king's wealthiest merchants and courtiers came by and simply walked around it. Many loudly blamed the king for not keeping the roads clear. But none did anything about getting the stone out of the way. Then a peasant came along carrying a load of vegetables. Upon approaching the boulder, the peasant laid down his burden and tried to move the stone to the side of the road. After much pushing and straining, he finally succeeded.

After the peasant picked up his load of vegetables, he noticed a purse lying in the road where the boulder had been. The purse contained many gold coins and a note from the king indicating that the gold was for the person who removed the boulder from the roadway. The peasant learned what many of us never understand. Every obstacle presents an opportunity to improve our condition in life.

If you are willing to improve your condition, change and implement a plan to pay yourself first, these are the simple steps to take. You must do a detailed budget (Appendix A) that includes provisions for adequate life, disability and health care insurance. Once having done that you must simply make a commitment to save 10% of all that you make. Your commitment to this simple plan will…

1.   **Release your enthusiasm and empower your relationships.**

2.   **Accept challenges, release apathy, and belief in self will be restored.**

3.   **Assert your leadership and have your youth renewed providing you the freedom to be all you can be.**

4.   **Help you set your priorities and establish pride in yourself.**

5.   **Help you crystallize your vision and to channel negative energy to worthy endeavors.**

6.   **Help you have positive thoughts that will create positive changes. Your success will be honored and assured.**

The great actress, Katharine Hepburn, said, *"You learn in life that the only person you can really correct or change is yourself. You were taught to blame your fathers, sisters, brothers, school, and the teacher…you can blame anyone, but never yourself. It is never your fault. But it is always your fault because if you wanted to change, you would. It's as simple as that."*

Chapter V

Spend it After You Pay Yourself First

HANS REICHENBACK
"If error is corrected whenever it is recognized as such, then the path of error is the path of truth."

The "spend it after" personality has the habit of always paying himself first. This person will always achieve financial independence...it's only a matter of time. Why?

The "spend it after" personality always **pays himself first** and then lives off the balance. It's from what is left over that the mortgage or rent is paid. What's left over pays the phone and utility companies, dry cleaners, taxes, dentist, and grocery store.

Have you heard the old expression, "the rich get richer and the poor get poorer?" Now you know why! It's simply that the rich have formed good habits and pay themselves first, and the rest of the world does not.

Can anyone become rich? Yes, of course they can. All it takes is time and money. We all have some of both... it's what we do with them that counts. Some people have told me that it's no use because it would take them five years just to accumulate their six months of expense requirement, let alone to begin investing. Where will you be in five years if you don't begin now?

There is no magic bullet, no instant formula for success, but there is a success formula that works for everyone, over time. Pay yourself first just like wealthy people do, and before you know it, you'll get the same results they have gotten. Bad habits are easy to form but hard to live with, while good habits are hard to form but a pleasure to live with. Your life can be free of financial worry and achieved as easily as you got dressed this morning...by forming good habits!

Children are more fortunate than adults when it comes to learning new things, as they only have to learn them. As adults, we have to let go of what we already know and then let the new information in.

At the turn of the last century, Bishop Wright[1] of the United Brethren Church was discussing philosophy with a college professor. The bishop cited the facts that everything about nature had already been discovered and that all useful inventions had been made.

The professor politely told the bishop that he was mistaken. "Why, in a few years," he said, "we'll be able to fly through the air."

"What a nonsensical idea," the bishop said. "Flight," he assured the professor, "is reserved for the birds and angels." Bishop Wright was the father of two young budding inventors named Orville and Wilbur!

Many of you have grown up in families with members like Bishop Wright and are handicapped by the ideas you have learned there. The Wright brothers were able to overcome their limiting conditioning, and you can too.

Let's let go of what we already know and consider this. If you pay yourself the first 10% of what you receive each week and tenaciously invest, you will achieve financial independence. That's the only way to enjoy the great but elusive benefit leading to a worry-free life.

Pay yourself the first 10%. If you take home $200 per week, that's $20 and represents four hours' work based on a 40-hour week. If you earn $4,000 per week, save $400 representing the same four hours of work. In five short years, which is only 60 months or 240 weeks, by investing $20 each week at 10%, you'll have $6,715 which represents almost 34 weeks of your take-home pay. Your nest egg will be $80,587, if you save $400 per week.

The chart on the next page will help you see the benefit you can create at other income levels. In every event, by investing 10% of your take-home pay, if you can earn 10% compounded (and there is no guarantee you will), in five short years you will have accumulated almost 34 weeks or over eight months of take-home pay.

Weekly Take-Home Pay	Save 10%	Value Compounded @ 10% for 5 yrs.	# of Weeks of Take-Home Pay
$200	$ 20	$ 6,716	34
$400	$ 40	$13,431	34
$600	$ 60	$20,147	34
$800	$ 80	$26,862	34
$1,000	$100	$33,578	34
$1,200	$120	$40,294	34
$1,400	$140	$47,009	34
$1,600	$160	$53,725	34
$1,800	$180	$60,440	34
$2,000	$200	$67,156	34
$3,000	$300	$73,872	34
$4,000	$400	$80,587	34

Whether 10% of your take-home pay is $20 or $200, by following the "pay yourself first" rule, you'll have almost 34 weeks (over eight months) of take-home pay accumulated in just five short years assuming you earn 10% after tax compounding. There is, of course, no guarantee that you will achieve these investment results.

The next chart demonstrates the payoff of forming good habits over time, and will help you better understand why even Einstein was amazed. If you are in the habit of saving 10% for five years, 60 months, 240 consecutive weeks, it's a walk in the park to continue to do the same thing for another five years.

Note that although you have doubled the time you save 10%, the number of weeks of take-home pay saved increases two and one-half times. This is the miracle of compounding interest and is understood by all financially free people.

Weekly Take-Home Pay	Save 10%	Value Compounded @ 10% for 10 yrs.	# of Weeks of Take-Home Pay
$200	$ 20	$ 17,531	87
$400	$ 40	$ 35,062	87
$600	$ 60	$ 52,594	87
$800	$ 80	$ 70,125	87
$1,000	$100	$ 87,656	87
$1,200	$120	$105,187	87
$1,400	$140	$122,718	87
$1,600	$160	$140,249	87
$1,800	$180	$157,781	87
$2,000	$200	$175,312	87
$3,000	$300	$192,843	87
$4,000	$400	$210,374	87

Whether 10% of your take-home pay is $20 or $200, by following the "pay yourself first" rule, you'll have 87 weeks (over one year) accumulated in just 10 short years assuming you earn 10% after tax compounding. There is, of course, no guarantee that you will achieve these investment results.

Success depends on staying power. Lack of perseverance is the reason most people fail in business, in financial matters, and in their personal lives. The perseverance of Thomas Edison, through more than 10,000 failed experiments, gave us the electric light, and many other wonders of our age. The perseverance of Abraham Lincoln through nine political defeats won him the Presidency of the United States. The perseverance of the Colorado River made the Grand Canyon.

Chapter VI

The Great Crossover

ANONYMOUS

"Insanity is doing the same thing over and over again while expecting a different result."

Most people today are not getting what they want from their jobs, from their families, from their religion, from their government, and, most importantly, from themselves. Something is missing in most of our lives. Part of **what's missing is purpose, for part of our purpose is to be free**.

Instinctively, humankind has struggled to free itself from suppression and bondage, as is recorded in the history of our world in all its cultures. Dependency has always bred discontent leading to resentment and ultimately to the rebellion of those who have been dependent. At the core of the behavior of each, eventually rebellious child, is the resentment of his dependency on the parent.

In a world without financial freedom and meaningful values, what do we have to share but our emptiness? Most of us scramble about seeking distraction in music, television, people, sex, food, alcohol and drugs. Most of all, we seek things. Things to wear. Things to do. Things to fill the emptiness. Things to medicate the ever-present pain of our eroding sense of self and that never-ending desire to be free. Things to which we can substitute meaning and significance in life.

We've become a world of things, and most people are being buried in it, feeling empty, unhappy, and not knowing why.

What most people need, then, is personal financial freedom. Coupled with living in a free democratic country, personal freedom can be used to create a place of family and community that has meaning and purpose.

The generally disorganized thinking that pervades our culture has led us to default on decisions that affect ourselves, our families and our community to bureaucrats in far-off places who neither know us nor the quality of life issues that we and our communities face. Personal financial freedom allows us to become organized and clearly focused on specific worthwhile results.

By embracing and committing to change destructive financial habits, self-discipline, and undaunting persistence in your pursuit of personal financial freedom, you will throw off the chains of dependency and win back your personal freedom. You will feel pride from being what you are…the backbone of enterprise and action…**of being what you are intentionally instead of accidentally.**

Embracing personal freedom and reclaiming it as your own will allow you to replace the feeling of home most of you have lost. You can then make it part of that place of community that you want for yourself and your loved ones. It can become that place where words such as **integrity, intention, commitment, vision,** and **excellence** can be used as action steps in the process of producing a worthwhile result.

While it is politically incorrect to teach values through the perennial philosophies of the Hindu, Buddhist, Zoroastrian, Janist, Jewish, Shinto, Native African, Native American, Muslim, Bahai', Sikh, or Christian teachings, which contain, perhaps, the greatest "how to live" principles of the world, once personally free, you can now take back your community or neighborhood by teaching the essence of each. No culture, self-interest group, or government watchdog would object to teaching the guiding principles of ...

Responsibility	Respect
Deliberateness	Compassion
Initiative	Adaptability
Perseverance	Honesty
Optimism	Trustworthiness
Courage	Loyalty

Teaching these principles will give all citizens of your community a sense that their home is a special place, created by special people, doing what they do in the best possible way.

If you're now committed to changing your existing and enslaving bad habits, all you need is a plan, so let's get started.

What's the **difference between a habit and an addiction?** I'm sure there is one but not being a psychiatrist or physician, I'm not qualified to distinguish. They do, however, call them "the drug habit, drinking habit, gambling habit."

We said before: "Bad habits are easy to form but very hard to live with...Good habits are hard to form but very easy to live with."

Think about any bad habit you have and look at the difficulty it causes in your life right now. One of mine is not leaving enough time to get to an appointment. This causes me to speed, run through amber lights, lay on the horn when a slower driver is in front of me in a no-passing zone and causes people to think I'm rude.

Physically, not leaving enough time causes my blood pressure and pulse rate to rise off the charts, my adrenal glands to fill my blood system with enough adrenaline to fight a saber-toothed tiger, and, at the end of the day, I'm physically, mentally and emotionally exhausted.

Stress, physical, mental and emotional, is thought by many medical authorities to be the primary cause of over 90% of all disease. This is called psycho (of the mind) somatic (in the body) disease. In spite of my knowing all of this, I still often don't leave early enough to get to an appointment on time. Why?

Simply stated, habits are hard to break. A baby is much better off than you and I because a baby just has to learn. We have to change old habits, and only then can we implement new ones.

You must learn to pay yourself first. Remember when you took your first step, first rode a two-wheel bicycle or drove a car? You knew what to do and how it was supposed to be done but what happened the first time? Whatever the result was, you didn't quit and today you know how to do it effortlessly because you formed the habit.

If you will force yourself to pay yourself first every week for 21 weeks, the experts tell us you'll have formed a new habit. Exactly how much to save weekly we'll deal with later, but try to start with 10% of what you take home.

If you work 5 days each week, Monday through Friday, and you take what you earn Monday morning, you would be saving 10%. The other four and a half days you can continue to work for someone else, the mortgage company, dry cleaners, grocery store, orthodontist, utility company...but Monday morning must be yours.

As mentioned in Chapter II, when completing your budget (Appendix A), a part of your income must be allocated to take care of your life, health, and disability insurance needs. By so doing, if you die too soon to take care of your responsibilities, you'll have an instant estate through insurance to do it for you.

Unforeseen medical cost will not cause a setback or, worse yet, bankruptcy. You will have transferred that responsibility to a health insurer by paying a monthly premium. If, through accident or sickness, you lose your ability to work, an insurance company will send you a monthly check so the plan launched to get you to independence can be completed.

Welcome to the "great crossover" where you leave those self-destructive financially enslaving habits behind. Remember, only in America do we order double cheeseburgers, large fries, and a diet coke. We also continue to buy hot dogs in packages of ten and buns in packages of eight.

Not everything we do in this country makes sense, but once the habit has been formed, it is difficult but not impossible to change.

Chapter VII

What Do I Do With The Money?

GALILEO

"You cannot teach a man anything. You can only help him discover it within himself."

What would you do if you had these three choices? The first choice is a savings account that pays you five and one-half percent interest. The second choice is a money market account that pays you four percent. The final choice is a huge can with a lid that weighs 250 lbs. and a slit in the top just wide enough for you to slip your money in and pays no interest.

Let's assume that you're going to pay yourself first everything you earn on Monday morning. At lunch on Monday, you can go to the bank and deposit your 10% in the savings account or the money market. Alternatively, you can go to your 250-lb. lidded can in the vault and slip your 10% through the slit in the top.

At the end of five years, which account will have the most money? If you're a "spend more than you make" or "spend all that you make" personality, you probably guessed wrong because you probably said, "the five and one-half percent savings account."

In a way, human beings behave like bees[1]. If you place several bees in an open-ended bottle and lay the bottle on its side with the base toward a light source, the bees will repeatedly fly toward the light at the bottom of the bottle. It never occurs to them to reverse gears and try another direction. Being trapped in a bottle is an entirely new situation for them, one their genetic programming is not prepared for. As a result, they are unable to adapt to a changing environment.

Fortunately, we human beings are not preprogrammed. We are endowed with the intelligence to adapt. In fact, scientists conclude that as a species, it is our superior ability to adapt to virtually all environmental conditions that has allowed humans to emerge as dominant rather than the dinosaurs.

The can with the 250-lb. lid that pays no interest would have the most because you would not have been able to get it out. **Paying yourself first isn't enough. You have to change destructive old habits by leaving it there and never touching it.**

We know that AARP statistics show 80% of all those who are retired today have less than $600 in cash assets. That the median net worth of older households was $86,300 and the median value of homes owned by older persons was $78,900. As disheartening as these statistics are, they show that home ownership, which forces people to pay their mortgage and leave money there, is responsible for more than 90% of the embarrassingly small net worth that retired Americans have today. **Financial freedom can only come when you put money away and leave it there.**

If you're in a "spend more than you make" habit, you'll have the tendency to use everything you put away because you're still spending more than you make.

If you're in a "spend everything you make" habit, you'll be tempted to use everything you put away because there is always the great vacation deal, or that new furniture, or the car whose price was so good you couldn't pass it up.

The can with the 250-lb. lid worked because you couldn't get the money out...you had to leave it there and not touch it. It's far more important that you pay yourself first and never touch it, than putting it in the highest paying investment and spending it too soon.

That's one of the reasons why, in addition to home ownership, 401K and IRA plans work so well. You can't borrow from an IRA, and even if you borrow from your 401k plan, you're forced to pay it back. You face tax plus a penalty if you take it out too early, which gives you plenty of incentive to leave it there. It's a 250-lb. lid designed by the IRS.

If you have the advantage of automatic payroll deductions at work, use it. If you are used to spending all you take home, or even more, automatic payroll deduction is fantastic for you. Automatic deductions work because the money is put away before you see it and eventually you make the mental adjustment and don't miss what you don't see.

One of the most important factors in achieving personal financial success is the willingness to try things out, to experiment and to test new grounds. In fact, this is the only way to learn and to progress—trial and error, trial and error, trial and success. You may make a couple of mistakes, but ultimately you'll find a way.

Instead of putting bees in a bottle, put in a couple of butterflies. Turn the bottle so it lies flat with its bottom toward a bright light. Within a few minutes, all the butterflies will have found their way out. They try all directions—up, down, toward the light, away from the light, often bumping into glass, but sooner or later they flutter forth into the neck of the bottle and out the opening to freedom. You can enjoy freedom too!

By determining to put the money aside and leave it there, you can enjoy all of the following, and even more.

1.   The joy of a long, comfortable, and totally worry-free retirement, with no compromise in lifestyle, and no real concern about ever running out of money.

2.   The ability to intervene meaningfully in the financial lives of your children during your lifetime, and to leave a legacy.

3.   The ability to fund, in whole or large part, the education of your grandchildren.

4.   The capability to provide quality care for your parents in their later years.

5.   The ability to make a meaningful legacy to a much-loved school, church, charity or other institution.

In the next 24 hours, your heart will beat 103,689 times. Your blood will travel 168,000 miles. Your lungs will inhale and exhale 23,240 times. You will eat, on average, over three pounds of food. Probably you will exercise about 7 million of your 9 billion brain cells, and speak 4,800 words. Not a single thought, word or action will carry you any closer to the financial freedom you want in life for yourself, your family or community, unless you begin now not only to save and invest, but to leave it there for your long-term goal.

Chapter VIII

Earn the Right to be an Investor

GANDHI

"People tend to forget their duties but remember their rights."

Regardless of your social and economic status, before you invest, you must earn the right by first "saving" six months of living expenses. That's right, six months of living expenses.

Just like becoming financially independent is different for everyone but the same for all, so is earning the right to become an investor. If your monthly living expenses are $2,500, then you must save $15,000 before you invest your first dime. If your monthly living expenses are $25,000, you must save $150,000 before investing. Why?

There are both emergencies and opportunities that come along in life, and to properly prepare for them you must have six months of income readily available. There are such things as layoffs, cutbacks of hours, and companies going out of business. Then there are unexpected illnesses and accidents that can prevent us from bringing home a paycheck. Then there is always the car that breaks down or needs to be replaced, and the furnace, air conditioner, water heater, dishwasher or refrigerator that just quits.

You know Murphy's Law, "If anything can go wrong it will, at the worst possible moment." And how about OToole's corollary which says, "Murphy was a bloomin' optimist." Stuff happens, and we have to be prepared to meet it as it occurs.

Why not invest and accumulate six months of expenses in stocks, bonds, or mutual funds, you may ask? Remember Murphy's Law? It never fails that, just when the emergency comes up, the market goes down 40%, and you have no choice but to sell at a great loss.

What is the difference between a saver and an investor? A saver puts money safely aside so that it will be there when needed, usually in a few years or less. As examples, down payment on a house, replacing the car, getting ready for next years vacation, or that emergency that's unknown but on its way.

An investor, on the other hand, puts his money at risk and wants it to grow over the long term of at least five years; ten years or more would be even better.

Savers have the benefit of knowing that all their money will be there when they need it. The cost savers pay for the benefit of certainty is relatively low interest, and they will normally have to pay income tax on the low interest earned. It may not be very exciting to save in a low-yielding account and may take years to meet the six-month minimum, but be patient. Where will you be years from now if you don't start this required emergency or liquidity fund today?

A painfully shy man fell in love with a young woman[1]. He sensed that she felt the same way, but he couldn't find the courage to ask her out. Finally he decided he would mail her a love letter every day for one year, and then ask for a date. Faithfully, he followed his plan, and at year's end he was courageous enough to call her, only to discover she'd married the postman.

Get your savings started today!

An investor, on the other hand, never knows how much money will be there at any given time, but knows that, over the long term, stocks usually do about twice as well as savings accounts. The informed investor knows that, in the short term, the value of the investment will go up or down each day.

Although we have limited our discussion to savings accounts and stocks, the same principles that apply to savings accounts apply to money market funds available at banks, credit unions and brokerage houses. When you want and need your money, although interest rates go up and down, your principal is there, all of it!

As with stocks, the same long-term principles and price fluctuation apply to bonds, mutual funds that own stocks and bonds, and even real estate. You never know what the value will be on any given day, but over the long term, these investments generally do better than all types of savings accounts (see chart on next page).

CD RATES VERSUS STOCK MARKET RETURNS (1970-1997)

Year	CD Rate	S&P 500*	Year	CD Rate	S&P 500*
1970	7.90%	3.94%	1984	11.17%	6.27%
1971	5.34	14.30	1985	8.54	31.73
1972	5.13	18.99	1986	6.70	18.67
1973	8.61	-14.69	1987	7.21	5.25
1974	10.43	26.47	1988	8.18	16.61
1975	7.11	37.23	1989	9.46	31.69
1976	5.76	23.93	1990	8.49	-3.10
1977	6.09	-7.16	1991	6.06	30.47
1978	8.95	6.57	1992	3.82	7.62
1979	12.03	18.61	1993	3.34	10.08
1980	13.75	32.50	1994	5.05	1.32
1981	16.93	4.92	1995	6.16	37.58
1982	13.28	21.55	1996	5.61	22.96
1983	9.65	22.56	1997	5.87	33.36

Source: Federal Reserve Board. The certificate of deposit (CD) rate is a six-month CD yearly average.
*The S&P 500 is an unmanaged index of 500 large company U.S. stocks.
While stocks incur more risk, CD's offer a fixed rate of return, and the interest and principal on CD's are generally insured up to certain amounts

Earning the right to become an investor may not be as exciting and pleasant as just jumping in and starting to invest, but it is critical for your long-term success. A guide at Blarney Castle in Ireland2 was explaining to some visitors that his job, like yours of saving, was not always as pleasant as it seemed. He told them about a group of disgruntled tourists he had taken to the castle earlier in the week.

"These people were complaining about everything," he said. "They didn't like the weather, the food, their hotel accommodations, the prices, everything. Then to top it off, when we arrived at the castle, we found that the area around the Blarney Stone was roped off. Workers were making some kind of repairs."

"This is the last straw!" exclaimed one person who seemed to be the chief faultfinder in the group. "I've come all this way, and now I can't even kiss the Blarney Stone."

"Well, you know," the guide said, "according to legend, if you kiss someone who has kissed the stone, it's the same as kissing the stone itself."

"And I suppose you've kissed the stone," said the exasperated tourist. "Better than that," replied the guide. "I've sat on it."

Now, don't you "sit on it." Get your six months of living expenses "savings account, emergency, opportunity or liquidity fund," underway right now.

Chapter IX

So Now You're an Investor!

ALFRED, LORD TENNYSON
*"That which we are, we are, and if we are ever to
be any better, now is the time to begin."*

Here are the basic rules. Over the long run, owners
do better than loaners. An owner is someone who forfeits
a guarantee in return for participating in the increasing value
of a venture, be it stocks, your own business or real estate.
A loaner has a guaranteed return of investment and interest
through such instruments as savings accounts, CD's, and
government bonds.

"How much better do owners do than loaners?" you
ask. Twice as well. "What is the long run?" you say. Ten
or more years. "Is it always true that the owners do twice
as well as loaners?" you query. Generally it is true, but
there are exceptions to every rule, so here is another important piece of information.

You can lose money by investing in the market, but
the longer you stay invested the better your odds are at
coming out ahead. Let's take a look at the U.S. stock and
bond market. There has never been a 20-year period when
an investor who owned a well-diversified portfolio of U.S.
stocks or bonds would have lost money. Let me re-
peat...never!   (See chart on the next page.)

The first bar in each section (stocks, bonds, cash) shows the highest and lowest returns using a one-year holding period. As you can see, in the best year of owning stocks, you could have made as much as 53% and, in the worst year, lost 42%.

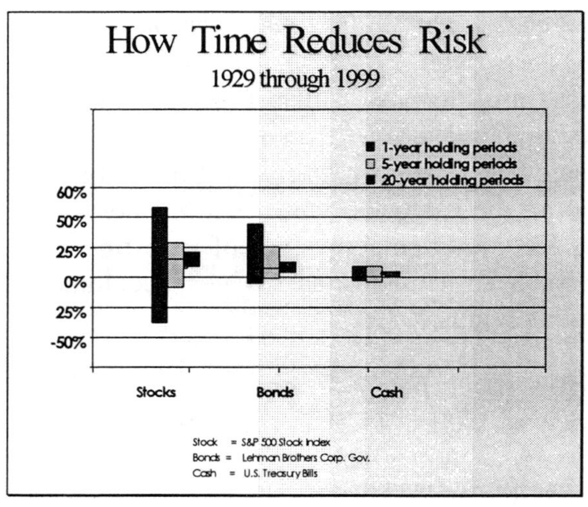

The second bar of each shows the best and worst returns with a five-year holding period. The last bar reflects historic results using a 20-year hold. The best 20-year stock holding period was 18% and worst, 4 %. Bonds and cash were similar.

Investors look forward to the future with faith, because they have observed the course of history and detected constant progress. Investors have noted the tendency of shares of great businesses to experience growth over time. Informed investors know their principal will fluctuate and, armed with faith, time and diversification, will probably continue to do twice as well as loaners in the future.

Does that mean if you invest now and stay invested for 20 years, you can't lose money? I didn't say that. Past performance can never guarantee the future and there is nothing in investing that can be absolutely guaranteed either. **Let's look again at the previous chart.**

As you can see from the previous chart, the longer you stay invested, the greater the opportunity you have for success, whether you're buying stocks or bonds. When investing, you can either be an owner or a loaner; that's always up to you.

Let's say you own a $100,000 CD at a bank. You have loaned the bank your money, which they in turn will loan out to someone who wants to own a home. Ten years later, the value of your CD with interest accumulated is probably going to be a lot less than the $100,000 home the borrower bought with your money.

In a similar way, when you own bonds you're loaning to corporations (except when buying U.S. government issues) whose stock in 10 years will probably be worth a lot more than your bonds with accumulated interest.

Loaners or bondholders are more secure and take less risk than owners so they get paid less but get paid back before owners or stockholders if there is ever a problem. So, depending on your age, need for income, and circumstances, you may want to be a total owner, a total loaner or somewhere in between.

As a general rule, when you are within ten years of a significant life event creating the need for money, you should have some of your money in stocks, some in bonds and a smaller amount in cash. A good rule is to subtract your age from 100 and the result is the percentage to have in stocks. This is the rule to follow if you are now reliant on the income from your investments or within ten years of relying on it.

What about investing for your grandchildren's education? Being a grandfather myself, it's a fine idea, provided you have enough income for yourself and can live with comfort for the rest of your life after adjusting for inflation and taxes. Over 30 years, I have encountered scores of parents and grandparents who simply can't afford to do what they would like to do for their children, both minor and adult, and their grandchildren. They're wonderful, well-meaning people who are not financially independent. Their children and grandchildren are often part of the many reasons why.

The best gift you can give a hungry person is not a fish but rather the lessons necessary to learn to fish and care for himself. As the story goes, "Give a man a fish and he'll eat for a day…teach a man to fish, and he'll sit on a charter boat drinking beer all day."

Seriously, the best gift we can give to those we love the most is to teach them to pay themselves first and lead by our own good example. Poverty is learned behavior as is being a "spend more than we make," "spend all that we make," or "pay yourself first and spend the remainder" personality. We don't inherit bad habits. They were inadvertently and unintentionally taught to us, usually by example. As you learn new information, lead by example, and although you may be initially unpopular, your family will benefit for generations.

If, in a financially responsible way, you can invest for your grandchildren's education, follow the same general rules as above, and the closer the child gets to needing the money, the more you should put in bonds. The mistake most investors make is always investing in bonds or CD's for education.

Let's say that you have a newborn grandchild and her name is Hailey Victoria (that's my newest and she is beautiful). Compare the results of the "Traditional Funding Chart," which assumes $5,000 is put away each year in bonds, to the "Sound Financial Funding Chart," which invests the same $5,000 in stocks for the first 13 years and then moves to bonds as the tuition bills draw nearer.

While there is no guarantee that you can average 6% on bonds or 10% on stocks, look at the result in 18 years when the first tuition payment comes due...a $37,742 advantage. (See chart on the next page.)

Education Funding Chart

Traditional Funding

Annual Payment	# of Years	Investment Rate	Value in 18 Years
$5,000	18	6%	$154,528

Total = $154,528

Sound Financial Funding

Annual Payment	# of Years	Investment Rate	Value in 18 Years
$5,000	13	10%*	$164,085
$5,000	5	6%	$ 28,185

Total = $192,270

*$5,000 annual deposit earns 10% for 13 years and compounds to $122,614. Then $122,614 is invested more conservatively at 6% for the next 5 years.

If you depend on investment income now, you still need stock in your portfolio to compensate for inflation. The average retiree who is 65 today will live another 20 years, and in that time will likely, even with moderate inflation, see the cost of living double. Remember going to a movie for $2.00, or mailing a letter for 20 cents?

The car you're driving will have to be replaced, the rent or taxes you're paying will go up and the trip to the restaurant or supermarket will cost more. There are only two ways to guard against this. First, spend only about half of the income you receive and reinvest the rest for the future. Second, have a percentage of your portfolio in stocks, which will grow at a rate greater than inflation and taxes.

Chapter X

What About Investment Taxes and Inflation

MARK TWAIN

*"What's the difference between a taxidermist and a
tax collector? The taxidermist only takes your skin."*

Over the past 30 years, I have observed two opposing
schools of thought on investments and taxes. One says capital gain at 20% federal plus state, if applicable, isn't so
bad, so pay your taxes along the way. The other says always
defer paying taxes until they must be paid.

Everyone, however, agrees that you should do as
much as possible to minimize the amount of tax that is
due. There are three basic choices...tax-free, tax-deferred
and taxable. In addition, some programs allow you a tax
deduction when you first deposit the money.

Tax-free investment choices are limited to municipal
bonds and Roth IRA's, if you qualify. Neither allows for
a tax deduction when the money goes in. For municipal
bonds, you must be a loaner and sacrifice the opportunity
for the double-digit returns often available through stocks.
However, for those in higher tax brackets, a tax-free return
of 6% would need to find a taxable equivalent return of
over 9% to do as well.

The Roth IRA does allow the potential for greater
returns because, if eligible, you can invest it in stocks or
mutual funds. The maximum allowable contribution is currently $2,000 each year; however, there are some restric-
tions, and higher earners cannot participate. Both Roth

IRA's and municipal bonds allow for totally tax-free distributions and should not be overlooked.

Tax-deferred, on the other hand, offers many more choices ranging from pension, profit sharing, IRA, 401K, 457, and 403b plans to the insurance industry's barrel of pork called deferred annuities. The banks have their barrel called FDIC Insurance and most banks, through their investment arms, also offer non-FDIC insured annuities.

The advantage of all the above tax-deferred accounts is that you pay no tax on the account until you take the money out and, as a result, you can change investments as often as desired without income tax consequence. If you think the stock market is headed for a crash next Friday, you can sell off and put all your money in cash until it's over and you're ready to return to stocks…and pay no taxes even though you may have enjoyed huge gains. Good luck in making accurate calls about market corrections like that!

The disadvantage with all tax-deferred investments is that when you take the money out, you forfeit long-term capital gain treatment, currently 20% plus state, if applicable and have to pay the higher ordinary tax rates, which currently range (for most of us) from 28% to 39.6% plus state, if applicable.

The two schools of thought mentioned at the beginning of this chapter have differing opinions as to what method of accumulating future wealth is best. Laws change over time and so do interest, inflation, and tax rates. The following chart will give you some idea of what has happened with interest, tax rates and inflation since 1970.

CD RATES VERSUS STOCK MARKET RETURNS (1970-1997)
(After tax and inflation)

Year	CD rate	S&P 500*	Maximum Tax	Inflation	Real Return Of CD's	Real Return of S&P 500*
1970	7.90%	3.94%	71.75%	5.57%	-3.16%	4.96%
1971	5.34	14.30	70.00	3.27	-1.62	0.27
1972	5.13	18.99	70.00	3.41	-1.81	1.53
1973	8.61	-14.69	70.00	8.71	-5.64	-12.58
1974	10.43	26.47	70.00	12.34	-8.20	-18.66
1975	7.11	37.23	70.00	6.94	-4.50	2.84
1976	5.76	23.93	70.00	4.86	2.99	1.25
1977	6.09	-7.16	70.00	6.70	-4.57	-9.15
1978	8.95	6.57	70.00	9.02	-5.81	-7.53
1979	12.03	18.61	70.00	13.29	-8.55	-7.97
1980	13.75	32.50	70.00	12.52	-7.46	-3.72
1981	16.93	-4.92	70.00	8.92	-3.53	-10.47
1982	13.28	21.55	50.00	3.83	2.71	5.05
1983	9.65	22.56	50.00	3.79	1.00	5.94
1984	11.17	6.27	50.00	3.95	1.57	-1.96
1985	8.54	31.73	50.00	3.80	0.45	10.32
1986	6.70	18.67	50.00	1.10	2.23	7.14
1987	7.21	5.25	38.50	4.43	0.00	-1.88
1988	8.18	16.61	33.00	4.42	1.02	5.53
1989	9.46	31.69	33.00	4.65	1.61	14.91
1990	8.49	-3.10	33.00	6.11	-0.40	-8.44
1991	6.06	30.47	31.00	3.06	1.09	16.57
1992	3.82	7.62	31.00	2.90	-0.26	1.63
1993	3.34	10.08	39.60	2.75	-0.71	2.55
1994	5.05	1.32	39.60	2.67	0.37	-2.49
1995	6.16	37.58	39.60	2.54	1.15	18.85
1996	5.61	22.96	39.60	3.32	0.07	9.58
1997	5.87	33.36	39.60	1.70	1.81	17.59

Source: Federal Reserve Board. The certificate of deposit (CD) rate is a 6-month CD yearly average. Taxes are federal taxes only andreflect the top federal tax bracket.
The Consumer Price Index is a commonly used measure of inflation.
* The S&P 500 is an unmanaged index of 500 Large Company U.S. stocks.
While stocks incur more risk, CDs offer a fixed rate of return and the interest and principal on CDs are generally insured up to certain amounts.

As you can see from the previous chart, interest rates fluctuated from a high of 16.93% in 1981 to a low in 1993 of 3.34%. Meanwhile, Federal taxes moved around too, with the highest rates of 71.75% in 1970 and a low of 31% in 1991 and 1992.

Another observation I hope you'll make from this chart is that inflation plays a very large role in your accumulating wealth. It is only what you have after taxes and inflation that counts. Many people were excited getting 12.03% on CD's in 1979, but failed to understand that with inflation at 13.29%, they lost 1.26% before they paid their taxes. Its easy to see why the stockbrokers often refer to CD's "as certificates of disintegration," but you still need them and other lower paying liquid investments for your emergency or liquidity fund.

You may have heard the expression, "Don't let the tax tail wag the dog." In other words, make good investment decisions and don't let the tax consequences keep you from doing what's right for you. Unfortunately, public policy and capital gain taxes keep us from making good investment decisions. Tax policy regarding investments discourages movement, especially short-term movement.

There are millions of people who have too many eggs in one basket and virtually no diversification because they inherited a lot of IBM shares or worked for a company where they acquired, over time, a lot of shares. These people know that, as good as their stock may be, there is more than one good game in town and they would be better off diversifying and owning shares in a number of good companies.

To do the right thing today costs 20% (the lowest in 30 years) plus state tax, if any, and keeps many very smart people from being diversified. Jim and Marie came to me in the early eighties, both having retired from IBM. Literally, all of their wealth and financial independence was tied to how that company did. Over the years, through payroll deduction, they acquired a great number of personal shares. Due to the tax consequences, they refused to sell, even when the Chairman of IBM appeared on the front page of the *Wall Street Journal* and said, "it would take a few years for IBM to work out its problems."

Jim and Marie watched the value of IBM fall from over $100 per share to less than $40, and their wealth evaporated overnight. Had they been willing to sell and diversify their holdings they would be much better off today, but the tax tail, at least in this case, wagged the dog.

Charles was an executive with a health care company. Over the years he acquired over $1,000,000 of the company's stock, and like Jim and Marie, knew he had too many eggs in one basket but refused to diversify, due to taxes and a belief that the stock value would always increase. A story appeared in *Barrons* that changed all of that. The stock plummeted from over $20 per share and today has been delisted from the NASDAQ and is trading for 18 cents per share.

Another lesson that I hope you'll learn from the stories of Jim, Marie, and Charles is the difference between well-established companies and new. Because Jim and Marie owned a "giant", which has proven over generations to be a good company, they are doing OK today, and their IBM did a turnaround. Charles, on the other hand, was involved with a new "small" company that went public and it doesn't look like it's coming back.

For serious investors, another lesson from history is to own a **diversified portfolio** of good companies through individual security selection, mutual funds, or annuities, and hold them for the long term (10 years or more). The **"Why Diversify Chart"**,(see next page) shows the importance of diversifying because no one category of investment does well all the time. Serious investors understand that it's impossible to know what category will do best next. By owning portfolios containing portions of each category, you can smooth out performance and do well over time.

WHY DIVERSIFY?
Growth Leadership Changes

Year	Large-Cap Stocks	U.S. Growth Stocks	U.S. Value Stocks	Small-Cap Stocks	Int'l Stocks	U.S. Bonds
1985	32.85%	33.31%	29.68%	30.97%	56.16%	22.11%
1986	15.36	14.49	21.67	3.58	69.44	15.30
1987	5.13	6.50	3.68	-10.48	24.63	2.75
1988	11.27	11.95	21.67	20.37	28.27	7.89
1989	35.92	36.40	26.13	20.17	10.54	14.53
1990	-0.26	0.20	-6.85	17.41	-23.45	8.96
1991	41.16	38.37	22.56	51.19	12.13	16.00
1992	5.00	5.06	10.53	7.77	-12.17	7.40
1993	2.90	1.68	18.60	13.36	32.56	9.75
1994	2.66	3.13	-0.63	-2.43	7.78	-2.92
1995	37.19	38.13	37.00	31.04	11.21	18.47
1996	23.12	23.91	22.00	11.26	6.05	3.63
1997	30.49	36.53	29.98	12.95	1.78	9.65
1998	38.71	42.16	14.67	1.23	20.00	8.69
1999	33.16	28.25	12.72	43.09	26.96	-0.82

Large cap measured by the performance of the Russell 1000 index... Small cap measured by the performance of the Russell 2000 index... International stock measured by the performance of MSCI EAFE index... U.S. growth measured by the performance of S&P BARRA growth index... U.S. value measured by the performance of the S&P BARRA/Value index... U.S. Bonds measured by the performance of the Lehman Brothers Aggregate Bond index... Securities indexes assume reinvestment of all distributions and interest payments and do not take into account brokerage fees and taxes. It is not possible to invest directly in an index. International investments are subject to certain risks, such as currency fluctuations, economic instability and political developments. Investing in small and midsize companies increases the risk of greater price fluctuations.

Why is it important to get steady, predictable returns rather than jumping all over the place? Take this quiz and let's see what you think. If you had $100,000 to invest for 10 years, would you rather get 8% every year or would you prefer these differing returns each year (20%, 21%, 10%, -16%, 12%, -2%, 22%, 6%, 11%, 15%)?

At the end of 10 years, which portfolio do you think would have more money in it? Which portfolio do you think would have taken more risk? Now that you have drawn your own conclusions, take a look at the "Tortoise & Hare Chart" on the next page.

Tortoise & Hare Chart

Starting with a $100,000 balance, which scenario of gains (+) or losses (-) will produce a high cash balance in 10 years?

Year	Scenario #1	Scenario #2
1	20%	8%
2	21%	8%
3	10%	8%
4	-16%	8%
5	12%	8%
6	-2%	8%
7	22%	8%
8	6%	8%
9	11%	8%
10	15%	8%

Again, let me ask…which portfolio do you think would have more money in it?

Scenario #1: Fund Value at End of 10 Years = $215,571

Scenario #2: Fund Value at End of 10 Years = $215,892

Steady, predictable results over time generally beat owning the "hottest securities," and the chart demonstrates why the wealthy look for steady and predictable results through asset allocation and diversified investment portfolios. The first rule of wealthy investors is "never lose money."

Form 1040_1 could easily have been called 1039 or 1041. The IRS has assured the American public that the number 1040 was a random selection. Still, some taxpayers insist its not a mere coincidence that in merry old England, Lady Godiva, dressed only in long hair, rode through Coventry protesting oppressive taxes in the year 1040. Don't let "the tax tail wag the dog," and remember that tax laws, as well as interest and inflation rates, change over time.

Chapter XI

I'm too Poor to Become Financially Independent

AZIE TAYLOR MORTON
> *In Spring 1980, in an auditorium packed with people standing along the walls, she said, "My mother was a deaf mute, I never knew my father, my first job was a cotton picker, and today I accept the post of the Treasurer of the United States of America."*

America 2000 is filled with people who have overcome the "I'm too poor" syndrome. There are millions who have come from poverty to financial independence, and there is nothing stopping you from doing the same. It doesn't matter how poor you may be, how hopeless your situation may now look or how many generations you and your family have been impoverished.

At age 7, United States Supreme Court Justice Clarence Thomas$_1$ went to live with his grandmother in Savannah. They lived in a one-room tenement sharing kitchen facilities with other tenants. His grandmother taught him how to work...the discipline, the sacrifice, and the sense of satisfaction at completion of projects. On scholarship to Holy Cross, Clarence studied for the priesthood and worked in the kitchen. He later earned his law degree at Yale. Clarence Thomas' life has been shaped by discipline, faith, and his own "power of positive thinking" to counter negatives that reaffirm failure in the minds of people.

In the United States, the only thing that can keep you from financial independence is yourself. It doesn't matter what your nationality or religion is. It doesn't matter who your parents were, and it doesn't matter how abused you have been, or how poorly you feel you have been treated up to now.

Marriott Hotels founder, J. Willard Marriott, was raised on a western sheep ranch where he was responsible for helping care for his eight brothers and sisters. Determined to get an education, he worked summers selling woolen goods, eventually building up a sales force of 45 college students who sold in seven states. "I have always felt that America is the land of unlimited opportunities for those who will pay the price. I also believe that one should choose a career with a future and then never give up no matter what setbacks he might encounter."

Since 1947, The Horatio Alger Association$_2$ of Distinguished Americans has been dedicated to honoring the accomplishments and achievements of outstanding individuals in our society who started with nothing and have succeeded in the face of great adversity. Their stories encourage people to pursue their dreams with determination and perseverance. I challenge you to read the " rags to riches" lives of these great people. If they were able to start with nothing and overcome such adversity, you can too!

Oprah Winfrey$_3$, a Horatio Alger member, at the 1999 National Book Awards, as part of her acceptance speech said: "I admire, respect and adore authors. My reading of *I Know Why the Caged Bird Sings* when I was a teenager was my first recollection of being validated.

The fact that someone as poor as I, as black as I, from the South, from rape and from confusion could move to hope, to possibility, and to victory...could be written about in a real book, that I had chosen in the library...was amazing to me."

In her July/August 2000 on-line magazine (*O Magazine*), in an article titled *What I Know For Sure,* Oprah says; "Once your personal boundaries have been violated as a child, it's difficult to regain the courage to stop people from stepping on you. You fear being rejected for who you really are. So for years I spent my life giving everything I could to almost anyone who asked. What cured me was understanding the principle of intention..."

What are your intentions? Do you intend to become financially free? Do you intend to create a legacy of pride and worry-free living for you and your family that will endure for generations? Couple these worthwhile intentions with the formation of new habits, and all that is required to succeed is time.

Here is all you have to do.

1.   You must pay yourself first.

2.   You must develop a budget and live by it.

3.   You must understand the law of Compounding
      Interest.

Eventually you will be financially independent. You must begin right now to pay yourself first...to put aside 10% of all you make and never touch it. As part of this step you must set up a debt repayment plan and live by it.

Alger Association member, H. Ross Perot[4], said, "Too many Americans have become credit junkies, shooting up borrowed money looking for another high. This country needs more men and women who can create new industries, new jobs, new capital."

Perot, the Texas billionaire with conservative ideas and political aspirations, was born the son of a horse trader. He always worked when he wasn't in school and eventually won free education at the Naval Academy. He joined IBM, quickly became a star salesman, and was then fired because he earned more than the chairman. He borrowed $1,000 in 1962 to start EDS (Electronic Data Systems). Follow his suggestion, give up the "credit card junkie" habit, pay off all existing debt and begin today to save 10% of all you make.

The second step, developing a budget (Appendix A), will assist you in this process. As you complete your budget, do it in a totally non-judgmental and non-accusatory way. It doesn't matter how bad the numbers look or who in the family is spending too much or on what. The only thing that matters is that it's accurate so you have a realistic place to start.

Please complete the budget in Appendix A before proceeding. Now that you see where your money is going, there are only two things, or a combination of both, that you can do. The first is to increase income. Remember, if you're in the habit of "spending more than you make" or "spending everything you make," this isn't going to help in the long run unless you change that habit (Chapters III & IV) because you'll soon increase expenses. The second alternative is to decrease expenses. Most effective of all would be to do both.

Decreasing expenses can be scary and it can make a lot of people unhappy because your lifestyle is going to change. Used clothes for the family instead of new by going to Goodwill and yard sales. One car, insurance premium and gas tank instead of many. Beans and rice instead of steak and potatoes. Videos and CD's from the local library instead of regular rentals and purchases at $15 each. There are thousands of ways to decrease expenses as long as your intention is strong enough and you really want to be financially free. Short-term pain, in exchange for long-term gain…a lifetime of worry free living for you and your family for generations to come.

Famous Amos Cookie founder, Wally Amos[5], born in Florida, was a poor youth who walked three miles to school for lack of bus money. Growing up in New York, he delivered newspapers and ice. At an age when most are contemplating retirement, he lost one fortune, one cookie company, but he rebounded and came up with an even better idea.

The kids starting paper routes, baby-sitting or other part-time jobs, provide various ways that many families have increased income. House cleaning for dual income affluent families is in great demand and pays $10 to $20 dollars per hour. The same is true of gardening and yard work. In general, those who are doing very well financially are desperately looking for people they can trust to do manual but well-paying work in and around their homes.

Carol Burnett[6] was born in San Antonio, Texas, to alcoholic parents who separated before she was 4 years old. She then lived with her grandmother and, with her wacky, warm-hearted humor and versatility, has won the hearts of millions of television viewers, movie buffs and live audiences around the world. Carol says, "Those who say they can't are absolutely right, and so are those who say they can."

You must do whatever is necessary to balance your new budget, which includes paying yourself first and retiring forever all your debt except your mortgage, if you have one. Our family found that we could cut the cost of going to a baseball game in half just by packing our own lunch and soft drinks. We didn't have to give up seeing the game and probably ate better, as well. There are as many ways to reduce expenses and increase income as there are stars in the sky.

Study the lives of Horatio Alger members, people from every background and situation who, because of their strong intention, changed their circumstances to benefit themselves, their families and communities forever.

Domino's Pizza founder, Thomas Monaghan[7], had a rough childhood. His father died on Christmas in 1941, when he was only four. His mother, a nurse, found herself unable to keep her job and raise her two boys, so she placed them in foster care. Thomas began studies at the University of Michigan, managing three newspaper delivery jobs to cover expenses. He and his brother managed to borrow $500 to buy Dominick's, a small pizza shop in Ypsilanti, hoping to pay his way through college. Eight months later, Monaghan traded a secondhand Volkswagen for his brother's share and started building what became the nation's largest chain of pizza stores.

The "Voice of Bell Atlantic," James Earl Jones[8], after overcoming a speech handicap, went on to his course of studies in drama. His first role was in an off-Broadway production, which paid little. He supplemented his income by polishing floors and working in a sandwich shop.

J.C. Penney[9] earned $4.27 a month as a dry goods clerk. When he was 22 years old, he moved to Colorado and opened a combination butcher shop/bakery. This business failed. After becoming a clerk in a clothing store, he was soon offered a partnership and an opportunity to open a branch store. In 1908, he bought out his two partners' three stores and soon opened two more. He was the founder and chairman of J.C. Penney Company.

CNN founder Ted Turner[10], who has given one billion dollars to the United Nations, knows what it means to grow up the hard way. Separated from his immediate family at age three, he lived with a grandmother for three years, and at age six was sent to a boarding school. At nine, he found himself enrolled at a military academy.

The table on the next page lists some of the other Horatio Alger members[11] about whom you may want to learn more. Just like Oprah Winfrey you can, without cost, go to your library and study the lives of these and other great Americans who have had the intention of bettering their lives and that of their families and their communities. Many have come before you without the benefit of great beginnings, and have overcome great obstacles, and have gone on to succeed. You can too!

Horatio Alger Association Members

Mary Kay Founder	Mary Kay Ash	McDonald's Founder	Ray Kroc
Amway Founder	Richard M. DeVos	34th U.S. President	Dwight D. Eisenhower
Pro Basketball Player	Julius W. Erving	38th U.S. President	Gerald R. Ford, Jr.
Boxing Champ	George Foreman	Miami Dolphins Owner	Joseph Robbie
Singer & Entertainer	Kenny Rogers	Golf Enthusiast	Bob Hope
Congressman	John D. Kemp	Secretary of State	Henry A. Kissinger
Wal-Mart Founder	Sam M. Walton	IBM Founder	Thomas J. Watson
Conductor & Entertainer	Lawrence Welk	Architect	Minoru Yamasaki
Evangelist	Billy Graham	Hallmark Card Founder	Joyce C. Hall
News Commentor	Paul Harvey	Hilton Hotel Founder	Conrad N. Hilton
Movie Star	Tom Selleck	Lord & Taylor Pres.	Dorothy Shaver
Entertainer	Danny Thomas		

Horatio Alger.com

Chapter XII

Solid Middle Class

GEORGE BERNARD SHAW
" Independence? That's middle-class blasphemy. We are all dependent upon one another - every soul on earth."

Many Americans feel that they would be better off making less because there is more aid available. With taxes, mortgage, health insurance, kids to the dentist, and college expenses it's impossible to get ahead.

Difficult...yes, but there is nothing that is impossible. You are dealing with some tough issues including taxes, and in 2000 the Tax Foundation, Washington, D.C., reported that the average American works until May 3rd...124 days...to pay costs of federal, state & local government: 10 - national defense, 9 - interest national debt, 19 - Social Security & Medicare, 39 - state and local taxes and regulations, 28 - federal regulation, 19 - other federal programs from peanut subsidies to foreign aid.

William J.H. Boetcker[1] said it all with his 10 points of common sense.

1.   You cannot bring about prosperity by discouraging thrift.

2.   You cannot strengthen the weak by weakening the strong.

3.   You cannot help small men by tearing down big men.

4.   You cannot help the poor by destroying the rich.

5.   You cannot lift the wage earner by pulling down the wage payer.

6.   You cannot keep out of trouble by spending more than your income.

7.   You cannot further the brotherhood of man by inciting class hatred.

8.   You cannot establish sound security on borrowed money.

9.   You cannot build character by taking away a man's initiative and independence.

10.   You cannot help men permanently by doing for them what they could and should do for themselves.

Looking at the bright side, common sense tells you there are 365 days in a year so you have 241 for yourself and you must use them very wisely. You must, like everyone else, begin with the basics and have six months of expenses put aside (Chapter VIII) and be saving 10% and retiring debt, other than your home mortgage, with 20% of your income.

A backward farmer$_2$, sitting on the steps of his shack, was approached by a stranger who stopped for a drink of water. "How's your wheat coming along?" asked the stranger.

"Didn't plant none."

"Really? I thought this was a good wheat country."

"Afraid it wouldn't rain."

"Oh. Well how's your corn crop?"

"Ain't got none," said the farmer.

"Didn't you plant any corn, either?"

"Nope, 'fraid of the corn blight."

"For heavens sake," said the stranger. "What did you plant?"

"Nothing," said the farmer. "I just played it safe."

The trouble is that being dependent on Social Security, Medicare, and the vast menu of government programs has made many Americans feel safe and instilled in many the feeling that the other guy will take care of it.

Ninety-three percent of retired Americans could not maintain their lifestyle if Social Security disappeared, and soon there will be only 2 workers to support each retiree versus 16 when the system started. Your children and grandchildren will be saddled with unbearable tax rates unless you take back personal responsibility and gain your financial independence now.

Begin right now. Anyone who has to make decisions regarding his financial freedom, just like the farmer, **cannot escape the tension** and emotional strain involved. Nor can he "just play it safe" by avoiding decisions. Inability to understand this has stopped many from moving forward, keeping them trapped where they are.

Change is always awkward and feels uncomfortable. Remember tying your shoes, playing a musical instrument or even driving a car for the first time? In order to enjoy the long-term gains of financial independence for you and your family, you must be prepared to endure some short-term discomfort. Change of any kind is always uncomfortable.

Turn to Appendix A and complete your budget, remembering it's far more important to be realistic than critical! You must begin with a clear understanding of where you really are right now. Imagine wanting to go to Mexico City and thinking you're in NY. You would have to travel southwest to get there. If you were really in San Francisco, rather than NY, traveling southwest would never get you to Mexico City. You must start out knowing where you are.

Now that you know where you are regarding income and expense, it's easy to do what needs to be done. You must increase income, reduce expenses, or use a combination of the two. There are no magic answers, easy ways or instant solutions. You must get your budget balanced after making provisions to pay yourself first at least 10%, and setting up a debt retirement plan requiring 20% of your income.

If the children have to work and don't have their own car, that's OK. If you have to go from two or more cars to one or perhaps even none that's OK too. Your family will be learning valuable lessons that will guarantee long-term financial security not only for them, but for future generations as well.

The message is you can achieve financial independence. You can educate your children, retire without fear of medical expenses or inflation, and live life with pride and dignity. To do this you must:

1.   Pay yourself first.

2.   Develop a budget and live by it.

3.   Work with the law of compounding interest.

4.   Develop a risk management program and stick to it.

Eventually you will be financially independent. How long will it take, you ask? That's up to you. Remember from Chapter II that financial independence is something that is different for everyone...yet the same for us all.

It's different for everyone because it's a function directly related to lifestyle. As said before, someone may be financially independent with an income of $25,000 per year while another may not be with $25,000 per month.

It's the same for everyone in that when you accumulate assets that generate enough income to fund your lifestyle, adjusting for both inflation and taxes, you're financially independent.

There are many of you who could be financially independent with $35,000 per year and just as many who need $75,000 to do the trick. Some of you will make dramatic adjustments in your budget and, as a result, could become financially independent immediately. Others will want to maintain the same life-style and, for you, it could take a lifetime.

What would be so bad about that...to have lived in the land of the free and to die truly free...financially independent? What a legacy you would be leaving future generations, what an awesome and inspiring heritage you would be creating for those who follow in your family. Chief Justice of the U.S. Supreme Court Clarence Thomas was the son of a sharecropper who was the son of a slave.

Chapter XIII

Affluence . . . Looking Good on The Outside

THOMAS JEFFERSON
"Never spend your money before you have earned it."
"Never buy what you do not want because it is cheap."
"Pride costs more than hunger, thirst and cold."

If your outflow exceeds your income then your up-keep will be your downfall. Affluence is a state in life that is denoted by high earners and even higher spenders. You live in nice neighborhoods, drive nice cars, wear nice clothes, eat in the best restaurants, and vacation in the most romantic places. For every dollar earned, you often spend more than a dollar and you make up a great number of people who others might think are wealthy.

As an affluent person, you are consumed by a lifestyle that can be just barely sustained on your high income, and prevents you from saving and investing adequate amounts for retirement. It is just a matter of time before disaster strikes. No lifestyle can go on forever without making adequate provisions for the future. The affluent are usually "spend more than you make", or sometimes "spend all that you make" personalities. Some save something, but not nearly enough for retirement, and find themselves totally dependent on Social Security and Medicare to sustain themselves in later years.

You have income that, if rechannelled, can quickly wipe out debt and have you on your way to financial independence. The missing ingredient is that you aren't paying yourself first or not paying yourself enough first, and must begin at the beginning with a budget. This will be especially difficult for you, because affluence means to flow freely and a budget means to flow only with purpose.

Ralph Waldo Emerson said: "Whatever you do, you need courage. Whatever course you decide upon, there is always someone to tell you that you are wrong. There are always difficulties arising that tempt you to believe your critics are right. To map out a course of action and follow it to an end requires some of the same courage that a soldier needs. Peace has its victories, but it takes brave men and women to win them."

Your personal financial freedom and peace of mind will be achieved with your perseverance and courage. Some of your high-living friends and neighbors will laugh, make fun of and probably stop associating with you. In the end, you will feel sorry for them; they will be worried and consumed by an out-of-control lifestyle. Your long-term rewards are great as you and your loved ones enjoy the freedom of financial security for generations to come.

Start by completing the budget in Appendix A. It's far more important to be realistic than critical! You must begin with a clear understanding of where you really are right now.

For the not-so-wealthy, affluent, who will be eaten alive by lifestyle and the inability to keep pace with inflation, you must begin now to:

1.   Pay yourself first.

2.   Develop and live by a budget.

3.   Invest wisely.

4.   Have adequate insurance and protect what you
       have.

5.   Give 10% away.

Just because you have a high income and perhaps
even a high net worth doesn't mean that you don't have
to begin to pay yourself first, and in a very serious way.
Based on the budget you have done, it is easy to see the
high cost of maintaining your current lifestyle. Just like
everyone else, if your outgo exceeds your income, then your
upkeep will be your downfall. Begin now to adjust your
lifestyle and save adequate sums of money to assure your
financial freedom.

Invest wisely and be sure to have an asset protection
program in place. In days of old, those who had assets lived
in castles surrounded by high walls and a moat. The only
way to enter was by crossing a drawbridge. People lived
that way because, without that protection, the barbarians
would take away what they had. In today's litigious society,
we still have barbarians who want to take what you have.
They wear pin stripe suits and are called "plaintiff's attor-
neys."

"Why should I give 10% away?" you ask. "You just
told me I have to reduce lifestyle and play catch up on
investments to assure my own financial freedom." Giving
away 10% is a critical step in assuring your financial freedom. Let me explain why.

There are many "tax-benefited giving strategies" that
may help you create more income for yourself (and your

spouse, if married) during life, leave as much or even a greater inheritance for your heirs (if that's important to you), and create a living legacy having a lasting impact on your community. While these strategies may not be right for you, investigate them with competent advisors or reputable not-for-profits…especially if you have capital gains tax issues. Worst case, as you give 10% of your income, your taxes will decrease.

For many years, Monterey, a California coast town, was a pelican's paradise[1]. As the fishermen cleaned their fish, they flung the offal to the pelicans. The birds grew fat, lazy and contented. Eventually, however, the offal was utilized, and there were no longer snacks for the pelicans.

When the change came, the pelicans made no effort to fish for themselves. They waited around and grew gaunt and thin. Many starved to death. They had forgotten how to fish for themselves.

The problem was solved by importing new pelicans from the south, birds accustomed to foraging for themselves. They were placed among their starving cousins, and the newcomers immediately started catching fish. Before long, the hungry pelicans followed suit and the famine was ended.

Seventy years of well-intended government programs have created a component of America 2000 who, like the Monterey pelicans, have forgotten how to care for themselves. There are no cousins to be brought in who remember how to fish because, unlike the pelicans, the government has put all these people…in every part of our nation…in housing projects, low income neighborhoods, and has their children going to public schools with other children from the same projects and economically depressed areas.

Robert Baker said: "Poor government comes about when good citizens sit on their hands instead of standing on their feet." You must stand on your feet and with 10% of your income, start to enjoy a tax deduction, and support non-profit organizations that are having a positive impact in helping people who have forgotten how to take care of themselves.

You must take back the responsibility for the quality of life in your community by your tax-deductible support of only those not-for-profits who are giving people a hand up, and avoid those who, although well intentioned (like our government), offer a handout.

Alternatively, there are a number of inexpensive ways to set up your own tax-deductible foundation and fund specific projects that you create in your own community. Most affluent are not ready for a foundation because they have a need for more income during retirement.

Many affluent people create trusts that allow them to avoid capital gains tax during life and pay them a supplemental income for life. At death, these trusts pay their proceeds to charities you selected, and replace their value to your family so those you love receive as much as if you had not given it away.

We rarely think of charitable giving as an alternative to paying taxes, for meeting social needs and creating more wealth for you. Yet **it is an alternative,** and often a better one. When you give one dollar in taxes to the IRS, you relinquish both the dollar and control over its use. It will go into the government coffers; from there, it will be split up among tens of thousands of communities and hundreds of thousands of people.

On the other hand, when you make a deferred gift of one dollar to a charity of your choice, for a program of your choice, you are exercising absolute control over its use and keeping it while you're alive and building more personal wealth. Ultimately, it will go directly to serve the people you choose, through the program you choose, in the community you choose.

The Mennonites consider it wrong to take pay for helping another human being. Instead, they say, " I will charge thee nothing but the promise that thee will help the next man thee finds in trouble." Someone during your life has helped you, and with your high earnings it's now time to design and support a non-governmental system that gets these people who have forgotten how to take care of themselves back on their feet.

You have the dual responsibility of finishing up on your own financial freedom (steps 1 thru 4) and at the same time (step 5 giving 10%) planting the seeds of lower taxes, less government control and helping others regain their ability to take care of themselves. The ten strongest two-letter words in our language are, "If it is to be, it is up to me."

Chapter XIV

For The Top 2%... The Wealthy

CHIEF SEATTLE

"Humankind has not woven the web of life. We are all but one thread within it. Whatever we do to the web we do to ourselves. All things are bound together. All things are connected."

As mayor of New York City, Fiorello La Guardia[1] liked to keep in touch with all the various departments under him. While presiding over court on a cold winter night a trembling man was brought before him charged with stealing a loaf of bread. His family, he said, was starving.

"I have to punish you," declared La Guardia. "There can be no exceptions to the law. I fine you $10." As he said this however, the mayor reached into his own pocket for the money. "Here's the $10 to pay for your fine which I now remit," he said.

"Furthermore," he declared, " I am going to fine everybody in this courtroom 50 cents for living in a city where a man has to steal bread in order to eat. Mr. Bailiff, collect the fines and give them to the defendant!"

The hat was passed around and the man, with a smile on his face, left the courtroom with a stake of $47.50.

Mayor La Guardia might fine us all today. The Census Bureau says we have over 12% of our national population living below the poverty level in America 2000. If increasing taxes and adding more government programs would solve the problems, it would have happened long ago. The day the "average American" finished paying for the cost of government moved from March 5th in 1940 to May 3rd in 2000.

A government that consumed all the money its citizens made for the first 64 days of 1940 has added another 59 days and gobbles up every penny the average citizen earns for the first 124 days of 2000. It treats symptoms, not problems. Ninety-seven percent of our criminal justice budget is spent on incarceration and building more jails. We know that an ounce of prevention is worth a pound of cure, but government ignores this important basic truth.

Having paid your enormous tax bills, it is not enough to sit back and feel that you have done your part. Delegation of responsibility to the government thru the payment of taxes has not worked. As Gandhi said: "People tend to forget their duties but remember their rights."

Look around at your community and notice the hospital wings, public parks, day-care centers, museums, theaters, universities and community colleges that have resulted from great people who, although not numbered among the "super rich," have taken personal responsibility and made your community a better place in which to live. It's up to you to build on that rich heritage, for no family, home, business, relationship, community or nation can long survive unless we put back more than we take out.

Elizabeth Noyce[2] was from Silicon Valley where her husband, Robert, began Intel. When the marriage ended, she left with four children and $40 million. She came to Maine in 1976 to heal and stayed to return the favor. She gave jobs.

She gave her community a library and a golf course. When she wanted to donate $1,000,000 to public television, Betty didn't write a check. She built five houses, employing architects and carpenters, and donated the money from the sales.

When Maine's banks got caught up in the merger fever and local businesses had trouble getting loans, Betty donated $7 million to found a new and now flourishing local bank.

When the bakery was on shaky footing and hundreds of jobs might have headed out of state, she bought it. When downtown Portland faced empty buildings, she bought them too. She began an indoor farmer's market.

"I just hope to make a little difference in my own community," she said. "Selfishly, I give where my donation will make my immediate environment safer, cleaner, brighter...I leave it to others to do as much as they can do in their communities. And that's the way the wider world improves."

At her memorial service it was said: "Elizabeth Noyce decided to use her wealth to give what others needed...work."

Those who built the hospital wings, parks and day-care centers in your community may not have been as well off as Betty Noyce. None may have ever appeared on the Forbes 400 list along with Bill Gates, Warren Buffet, Ted Turner or Ross Perot, but they had enough wealth to make a significant difference in their community. You can, too.

The wealthy in the U.S. pay taxes and Alexis deTocqueville in his 1848 seminal work titled *Democracy in America* understood...

- **government is a consumer, not a producer of goods.**

- **anything government gives it must first take from the taxpayer.**

- **government intrusion is very expensive because of the buildup of bureaucracy.**

- **government intrusion requiring economic participation by either taxpayer or consumer gradually brings slavery to Americans.**

In fact, deTocqueville said that, "The American Democratic experiment will succeed until the people realize they can vote themselves money from the public treasury... then it will collapse."

Our elected officials in our "representative democracy" understand that in order to stay in office they must "bring home the bacon" and satisfy their constituents. Any government that robs Peter to pay Paul relies on the support of Paul. We must take back our personal freedom and responsibility by creating a better system to satisfy Paul.

Whether it's deTocqueville in the 1840's or Joseph Schumpiter, author of *Capitalism, Socialism and Democracy* in the 1940's, we must heed their warnings. Schumpiter predicted the fall of Communism in Eastern Europe by 1980 and was off by only 10 years. He, like deTocqueville, also predicted that U.S. workers would vote in Communism.

What's the difference between Capitalism and Socialism? Who controls the means of production. What happens in the United States today without government intervention?

What business has come to your community without the enticements of tax abatements, subsidized loans, loan guarantees or outright grants? What university functions without government aid or grants for research? What medical research, bio-tech or pharmaceutical development takes place without government funding? When was the last time a major "social project," even a professional sports team arena, was constructed in your area without the benefit of "lower financing cost" funded by tax-free municipal bonds?

If government controls the means of production, then we have a socialist and not a capitalist society. You can change that by becoming proactive with what you do with your wealth and controlling it yourself rather than allowing government to decide how to spend your hard-earned money.

For example, 35 years ago the Jaycees got permission to go downtown in Indianapolis (then known as "Indian No Place") on Saturdays and shoot pigeons because the area was so deserted and empty, the pigeons were overtaking the city.

Through commerce and philanthropic gifts from a foundation created by Eli Lilly, the city was rebuilt and is now a model American city. It's the Amateur Sports Capital of the World with 35 amateur sports teams headquartered there. The Lilly Foundation paid their moving expenses.

The 1987 Panama Games were held there and the Lilly Foundation paid a great deal of the building cost required. The Lilly Foundation was the major contributor to the world famous Hoosier Dome or it would not have been built.

Lilly took control of his forgotten riches without giving up control of his assets during life, and you can too! If you could legally control more assets for life and direct the income from them to organizations you choose, would you? If you could direct how and where more of your tax dollars would be used, rather than giving up control of them, would you?

The Robert W. Woodruff Foundation, created by the former president of Coca-Cola, has done for Atlanta what Lilly did for Indianapolis. Emory University would not be what it is without six million shares of Coca-Cola contributed by Woodruff. The Robert W. Woodruff Art Center nestled in downtown Atlanta houses the Atlanta Symphony, the High Museum of Art and other cultural organizations.

Woodruff Park and Centennial Olympic Park, both owned by the city, received half of their construction cost from the Woodruff Foundation. Woodruff helped the American Cancer Society, the Boys and Girls Club of America and CARE relocate from Manhattan to Atlanta, giving each about $2,500,000.

What many wealthy people don't realize is that there is an answer to "how much is enough?" How much capital do you want to take care of yourself for life? How much capital do you want to leave each heir including your spouse? Whatever these amounts total, you must plan to leave more because your heirs will have to pay some estate tax.

Think of all your wealth as being in two pockets. In one pocket is your personal wealth. It's the money you spend to live, or save for your later use, or save to give to your heirs. In any case, it's money intended for you and your family.

In the other pocket is the rest of your wealth. It's money that will go to others beyond you and your family. For most Americans, this wealth is taken from them in the form of taxes. Look at the "Income and Outlays" pie chart, second to last page of your "1040 Forms and Instructions" booklet from the IRS. You will find that 62% of all federal government outlays go to fund social programs.

When you pay a tax, you participate in philanthropy, as 62 cents of every dollar goes to fund social programs. Bureaucrats in Washington who don't even know you, where you live or what's important to you or needed in your community, redistribute your wealth in accordance with their priorities. They "bring home the pork" to their districts, and completely ignore what is important to you.

By putting aside "enough" for yourself and family and then giving the rest away through your foundation or directly to responsible charitable organizations, you maintain control of all your money and direct it in accordance with your, rather than the government's, priorities.

As wealthy people, you must apply the wisdom that says…

1.   You can't take it with you.

2.	You can't give it all to your family because of transfer (estate) taxes.

3.	Government, through taxes, will redirect your wealth and fund social programs of government's choosing.

4.	You can choose to redirect your wealth and personally select the social programs you wish to fund.

5.	You are a Philanthropist...Voluntary or Involuntary Philanthropy... The choice is yours.

What lies in the future of America in 2000 and beyond? We said earlier that the definition of insanity was doing the same thing over and over again and expecting a different result. Has the great "capitalistic experiment" failed or is it about go through a "renaissance"?

Will government, which produces nothing and extracts all its revenue from its citizens, continue to grow and be required to fund even more social programs? Or will we, the citizens, embrace personal responsibility and take care of ourselves, our families and our communities?

Whether you're poor, middle class, affluent or wealthy, only change in your behavior can produce a different result. Only by regaining your self-confidence, lost in America since the Great Depression, and taking back personal responsibility, can change occur. You must show government by your actions that it is no longer necessary for everything in life, because individual initiative and neighbors helping neighbors can do a better job.

Taking the necessary steps for personal financial freedom for you and family has never been more important. You are capable of throwing off the chains of financial bondage that put you and your family at the mercy of government programs that have robbed you of your dignity and self-respect. You can free your children and grandchildren from the "imprisoning future tax structure" that will otherwise be required to maintain Social Security and other programs as the baby boomers retire and the number of workers decreases.

Those who are affluent, financially free or wealthy have an awesome part to play in personal community involvement, thereby eliminating the need of government to "fix the problems" that you can handle so much better, efficiently, and cost-effectively.

The only way to reduce our enslaving tax burden is to redirect the current tax you are paying from government coffers, where you lose both the money and control of its use, to worthy not-for-profits, personal foundations, or a variety of trusts where you will enjoy both tax benefits and the control of what is done with your money.

America did celebrate Tax Freedom Day (Appendix B) on May 3, 2000. That means the nation's average taxpayer had to work from January 1, 2000, to the 124th day of the year before earning enough money to pay for government...federal, state and local...and start spending money on themselves. The only way to reduce this enslaving burden is to take personal responsibility for yourself and your community.

Individual income taxes are still the largest component of the nation's tax bill, and you work, on average, fifty-one days to pay them. Another thirty days will be spent working to pay payroll taxes, which fund social insurance programs such as Social Security and Medicare.

Sales and excise taxes are less noticed by the public because they're collected a little at a time, sometimes directly from the consumer and sometimes from businesses. On average, Americans worked sixteen days in 2000 to pay them.

America will spend another ten days working to pay property taxes, levied primarily by local governments, though some states have significant property taxes. Twelve days of work will go to pay corporate income taxes which are initially collected from businesses but ultimately passed on to individuals. Finally, Americans will spend five days working to pay other business and miscellaneous taxes.

Before Social Security, the elderly poverty rate, according to the Social Security Administrations 1997 report, was 47.6%. Even after Social Security, the elderly poverty rate is 11.9% and that's not the percentage of our retired population living with dignity, self-respect, and in financial freedom…that's just the elderly who live below our national poverty level.

Government bureaucrats have established the national poverty level as well as the standards for minimum wages, housing, and public schools. These are all "other guy" standards that they and their families don't have to live by. Where is there any accountability?

What would happen if those who made the rules and established the minimum standards had to live by them? What would happen if all U.S. citizens, regardless of their current socio-economic position, had to live under the "minimum standards" for two years?

Government loves lotteries, so let's have one where every citizen, including "our lawmakers," if selected, would have to live by the established minimum standards, including the housing and neighborhood, with their children attending the same neighborhood public school. After two years, they could return to their regular environment. Would that create accountability and make a difference?

It has to start with you. By changing from a "spend more than you make" or "spend everything you make" to "pay yourself first and spend the rest that you make," you will achieve personal financial independence. It's just a matter of time.

For those of you financially independent, your next step is to assume an even greater degree of financial responsibility and help others do the same. The few of you who are wealthy have an unparalleled opportunity to benefit yourselves and families and, while doing that, set the stage for the very poor to achieve the independence you have grown to take for granted. Government programs, although well intended, have failed. Let us return to our roots and take personal responsibility in our own communities and engender positive change.

We have everything to be optimistic about. Fear of the future is counterintuitive. Like race hatred, somebody had to teach it to you because you'd never figure it out for yourself. Virtually all of us have had an illness, flu, pneumonia or other infection, that 60 years ago would have killed us. MRI's tell us things it would have taken exploratory surgery to find out even 10 years ago. Today's population over the age of 85 is growing five times faster than the overall U.S. population. In addition, we haven't begun to hear from biotech yet.

Technology? The microprocessor, an entire computer on a chip, mankind's most important invention yet, isn't 35 years old. My son went off to school carrying a Texas Instrument TI-30 scientific calculator. It cost $12.88 in a drug store...it has more computing power than existed on earth in the year 1950! Government's primary role has been to collect and distribute information; computers can now fill that function.

Already, more young Americans own investments than any other generation of kids. Liberty Financial, a Boston money-management firm, conducted a recent survey that showed 35% of 8th through 12th graders owned stocks, bonds or mutual funds. In 1993, just 10% invested. Prior to the '90's, investment ownership among sub-20-year-olds was essentially zero. Half of all American adults own stock, also an all-time high.

Freedom or bondage? The choice is yours, and freedom will require some very significant but not impossible changes on your part. George Bernard Shaw said: "The reasonable man adapts himself to the world. The unreasonable one persists in trying to adapt the world to himself. Therefore, **all progress depends on the unreasonable man.**"

America 2000 has many citizens who are reasonable and have adapted themselves to the world. We must overcome our apathy, complacency and low achievement drive in order to regain our freedom.

Sir John Templeton said: *"It has taken 1,000 years for the standard of living to double in the most advanced countries, yet it may double for the world as a whole in the next 20 years." Will the next 20 years be the best the world has ever seen, or will it be the "fall of capitalism and the return to socialism?"*

About the Author

Joe Murtagh, President of the SOURCE, has been assisting investors since 1970. He helped his clients build wealth during the '70's while witnessing wage and price freezes, the largest U.S. trade deficit in history, a plummeting stock market in 1974 and skyrocketing oil prices in 1979.

Entering the '80's, with the highest interest rates in history, Joe and his clients did well during the worst recession since the Great Depression, steep U.S. dollar declines, followed by the stock market crash of 1987. They finished the decade with recession fears mounting and the $500 billion Federal bailout of the Savings and Loan Crisis.

He and his clients continued to do well during the '90's in spite of the Persian Gulf War exploding, followed by record unemployment and significant tax decreases. They rode out the bear market of the mid-1990's and, through this publication date, are enjoying a bull market as we enter the 21st century.

Mr. Murtagh is a Certified Financial Planner, Chartered Financial Consultant, Chartered Life Underwriter, Accredited Estate Planner and Registered Investment Advisor. He has lectured widely on financial topics to CPA societies, Bar Associations and numerous professional and business groups. His first book, *Retirement Investing,* was a great success and Joe was recently selected by a national magazine, *Wealth,* to be featured in a cover story.

Joe lives in Goshen, NY with his wife and family and writes a bi-weekly article featured in the *Hudson Valley Business Journal.* Copies are available.

How to Contact Us, Questions?

I would be delighted to answer any questions that we may not have covered in the book.

If you need help with investment or financial planning, I will try to assist you.

Call or write down your questions and fax, mail or email them to me, or contact me at our Web site *www. gotothesource.com.* I may have some brochures or booklets I would be glad to send on the topics that concern you.

Joe Murtagh
President
the SOURCE
99 Route 17A
Goshen, NY 10924

Phone: (845)   294-8383
       (800)   239-0058
Fax: (845)   294-2007

www.gotothesource.com

Appendix A
Budget

Annual Gross Income ________________

Fixed Expenses		**Variable Expenses**	
Housing (Mortgage/Rent)	________	Vacations & Travel	________
Utilities & Telephone	________	Recreation & Entertainment	________
Food, Groceries, etc.	________	Household Furnishings	________
Clothing & Cleaning	________	Education Fund	________
Income Taxes	________	Savings	________
Social Security	________	Investments	________
Real Estate Taxes	________	Other Expenses	________
Transportation	________	**Total**	________
Medical/Dental Expenses	________		
Debt Repayment	________		
Housing Supplies/ Maintenance	________		
Property/ Car/Liability Ins.	________		
Life/Medical/ Disability Ins.	________		
Current School Expenses	________		
Total	________	**Grand Total**	________

Appendix B

Tax Freedom Day
May 3, 2000

Year	Tax Freedom Day	Total Taxes as a Percentage of Income
1935	Feb 26	15.3%
1940*	Mar 5	17.6%
1945	Apr 1	24.7%
1950	Mar 31	24.5%
1955	Apr 3	25.4%
1960*	Apr 11	27.8%
1965	Apr 9	26.9%
1970	Apr 19	29.8%
1975	Apr 18	29.4%
1980*	Apr 21	30.5%
1985	Apr 19	29.8%
1990	Apr 22	30.6%
1995	Apr 25	31.5%
2000*	May 3	33.8%

*Leap year makes Tax Freedom Day appear a day earlier.

Footnotes

Chapter I
    1 aarp.com
    2 taxfoundation.org
    3 crystalcathedral.com

Chapter II
    1 aarp.com
    2 "The Best of Bits & Pieces", page 7*
    3 aarp.com

Chapter III
    1 *"Leadership"* September 23, 1997, pages 9 & 10*
    2 *"Leadership"* September 23, 1997, pages 14 & 15*

Chapter IV
    1 *"Leadership"* September 23, 1997, pages 23 & 24*
    2 King and Bolder

Chapter V
    1 *"Leadership"* November 16, 1999, page 5*

Chapter VI
    None

Chapter VII
    1 *"Leadership"* May 6, 1997 pages 15 & 16*

Chapter VIII
    1 "Good Stuff" page 2
    2 "The Best of Bits & Pieces" page 44**

Chapter IX
    None

Chapter X
    1 "The Best of Bits & Pieces" page 179**

Chapter XI
  1 horatioalger.com
  2 horatioalger.com
  3 oprah.com
  4 thru 11 horatioalger.com

Chapter XII
  1 "The Best of Bits & Pieces" pages 26 & 27**
  2 "The Best of Bits & Pieces" pages 64 & 65**

Chapter XIII
  1 "More of the Best of Bits & Pieces" page 62***

Chapter XIV
  1 "The Best of Bits & Pieces" page 102**
  2 "*Leadership*" November 16, 1999, page 5*

     AARP 3200 E. Carson Street, Lakewood, CA 90712, 800-424-3410

     Tax Foundation 1250 H Street NW, Suite 520, Washington, DC 20005, 202-783-2760

     Robert Schuller Center, 13280 Chapman Drive, Garden Grove, CA, 714-941-4000

     The Horatio Alger Association, 99 Canal Center Plaza, Alexandria VA 22314, 703-684-9444

     *Cited in "*Leadership*" The Economic Press, Inc., 12 Daniel Rd, Fairfield, NY 07004-2565; Phone: 800-526-2554, FAX 973-227-9752. E-Mail: *infor@epinc.com* Web site: www.epinc.com

**Cited in "The Best of Bits & Pieces" copyright 1994, The Economic Press, Inc., 12 Daniel Road, Fairfield, NJ 07004-2565; Phone: 800-526-2554, FAX 973-227-9752. E-Mail: *infor@epinc.com* Web site: www.epinc.com

"Good Stuff" PO Box 3019, Malvern, PA 19355-9617, 800-220-5000

***Cited in "More of The Best of Bits & Pieces" copyright 1997, The Economic Press, 12 Daniel Road, Fairfield, NJ 07004-2565, 800-526-2554; Phone: 800-526-2554, FAX 973-227-9752. E-Mail: *infor@epinc.com* Web site: www.epinc.com

Oprah Winfrey, Harpo Productions, 110 N. Carpenter St., Chicago, IL 60607, 315-633-0808